Roy (Lord) Hattersley is a Labour peer and former Deputy Leader of the Labour Party. He is the author of *David Lloyd George: The Great Outsider*; *Borrowed Time: The Story of Britain between the Wars*; *In Search of England*; *The Edwardians* and *50 Years On: A Prejudiced History of Britain since the War*.

Kevin Hickson is Senior Lecturer in Politics at the University of Liverpool. His publications include *Labour's Thinkers: The Intellectual Roots of Labour from Tawney to Gordon Brown* (with Matt Beech); *The IMF Crisis of 1976 and British Politics* (both I.B.Tauris); *The Struggle for Labour's Soul: Understanding Labour's Political Thought since 1945* (edited with Matt Beech and Raymond Plant); *New Labour, Old Labour: The Wilson and Callaghan Governments 1974–1979* (edited with Anthony Seldon) and *British Party Politics and Ideology after New Labour* (edited with Simon Griffiths).

'Slump, caused by financial-market excess and prolonged by "consolidation" policies of governments, is increasing disparities of income, opportunity and care; disabling economies and enfeebling democracies. As the thoughtful essayists gathered together in this book show, all those and other realities make *The Socialist Way* the practical, necessary and enlightened alternative to a future of stagnation, injustice and insecurity for millions here and across the world.'

– Neil Kinnock, former leader of the Labour Party

'Never mind the terminology – socialist or social democrat – amid the ruins of failed free-market extremism, new thinking is essential. Strong ideas attract voters, while the cynicism of "third way" floating-voter wooing turns people away. Here is flesh for Labour's One Nation principles, where rights and responsibilities apply to rich as well as poor, undeserving profiteering is marked out from worthwhile enterprise and the economic disaster of growing inequality shows fairness is the Scandinavian route to both growth and wellbeing. Clear thinking and optimism in these writings light the way ahead.'

– Polly Toynbee

'Free-market capitalism is in crisis, but the Left remains in an even bigger mess. There's a desperate need to renew the Left, and this book is a crucial contribution to doing just that.'

– Owen Jones, author of *Chavs: The Demonization of the Working Class*

'Labour is considering afresh the vision it will offer Britain under the next Labour government. This book fleshes out the thinking that will design and lead the policies within our next manifesto. It is essential reading for all who care about the Labour Party and the future we will build post-2015.'

– Madeleine Moon MP

'It is now time for Labour to revive the basic principles that we should never have discounted during the era of New Labour, but which are essential to facing the huge task we will take on in 2015: the rebuilding of a fair society in a strong nation. One nation back on the social democratic road. This book provides the route map for the revival of democratic socialism in Britain.'

– Austin Mitchell MP

'It's great to welcome a book that's not afraid to make the case for socialism, for equality and for strong and effective public services. As Ed Miliband fleshes out the detail of the Labour vision for One Nation, this publication offers great food for thought.'

– Kate Green MP, Shadow Minister for Equalities

'Throughout its history the Labour Party has faced the challenge of reinventing its programme for government whilst staying true to its values and moral purpose. This book is an important contribution to how Labour can do that under Ed Miliband's leadership, continuing further the debate about the direction and policies of One Nation Labour.'

– Jonathan Reynolds MP, PPS to Ed Miliband

'This book is a must read – and sets out important thinking for Labour as it frames its manifesto for the next election. It captures the very best of history, and applies the principles of democratic socialism in determining a vision for a fairer future in Britain.'

– Seema Malhotra MP

'*The Socialist Way* offers an important contribution to the debate over what place social democratic ideals have in today's Labour Party as, in opposition after 13 years in government, it looks to its long-term vision for the country. The range of viewpoints represented in this book, as well as the quality of its contributors, show that the principles that have always formed the backbone of the Labour movement remain alive and well.'

– Paul Farrelly MP

'This is an important contribution to the debate as we seek to formulate alternatives to the failed austerity agenda of the Coalition.'

– Dame Margaret Beckett MP

'Given the failure of the Coalition's austerity agenda, Labour needs to articulate its traditional values confidently and in a way that resonates with voters. This book offers plenty of ideas about how to do just that.'

– Bill Esterson MP

the socialist way

social democracy in contemporary Britain

edited by
Roy Hattersley
and **Kevin Hickson**

I.B. TAURIS

LONDON · NEW YORK

Published in 2013 by I.B.Tauris & Co. Ltd
6 Salem Road, London W2 4BU
175 Fifth Avenue, New York NY 10010
www.ibtauris.com

Distributed in the United States and Canada Exclusively by Palgrave Macmillan
175 Fifth Avenue, New York NY 10010

ISBN: 978 1 78076 580 8

A full CIP record for this book is available from the British Library
A full CIP record is available from the Library of Congress

Library of Congress Catalog Card Number: available

Typeset by Newgen Publishers, Chennai
Printed and bound by CPI Group (UK) Ltd, Croydon, CR0 4YY

MIX
Paper from
responsible sources
FSC
www.fsc.org   FSC® C013604

Contents

PART II. A SOCIAL DEMOCRATIC SOCIETY

PART III. A SOCIAL DEMOCRATIC STATE

PART IV. SOCIALIST INTERNATIONALISM

PART V. WINNING THE ARGUMENT

List of Contributors

Andy Burnham is MP for Leigh and Shadow Secretary of State for Health

David Coats is a research fellow at the Smith Institute and Director of WorkMatters Consulting

John Denham has been the Labour MP for Southampton Itchen since 1992 and is a former cabinet minister

Helen Goodman has been Labour MP for Bishop Auckland since 2005

Peter Hain has been Labour MP for Neath since 1991 and is a former Cabinet Minister

Andrew Harrop is General Secretary of the Fabian Society

Roy Hattersley was Deputy Leader of the Labour Party from 1983 to 1992 and is a Labour peer

Kevin Hickson is Senior Lecturer in British Politics at the University of Liverpool

Paul Hunter is Head of Research at the Smith Institute

William Keegan is the *Observer*'s senior economics commentator

Helena Kennedy is a civil rights lawyer and a Labour peer

Bill Kerry is Secretary of the Equality Trust

Peter Kilfoyle was Labour MP for Liverpool Walton between 1991 and 2010 and a former Defence Minister

Stewart Lansley is a visiting fellow of the Townsend Centre for International Poverty Research at the University of Bristol

Ruth Lister is Professor Emeritus of Social Policy at Loughborough University and a Labour peer

Arlene McCarthy is a Labour MEP for North West England and is Vice Chair of the Committee on Economic and Monetary Affairs

Michael Meacher is Labour MP for Oldham West and Royton and a former Minister of State for the Environment

David S. Moon is Lecturer in Politics at the University of Liverpool

Lisa Nandy is MP for Wigan and is Shadow Junior Minister for Education

Robert M. Page is Reader in Democratic Socialism and Social Policy at the University of Birmingham

Raymond Plant is Professor of Political Philosophy and Jurisprudence at King's College London and a Labour peer

Pete Redford is a PhD student at the University of Birmingham and Labour Party activist

Simon Slater is Deputy Leader of the Labour Group on Solihull Council

Andrew Vincent is Professor Emeritus at the University of Sheffield and Honorary Professor at Cardiff University

David Walker is contributing editor to the Public Leaders Network

THE SOCIALIST WAY

Roy Hattersley

There was a time, during the years of New Labour's greatest popularity, when it was fashionable to make jokes about what was derisively called 'the vision thing'. In part the jibes were directed, with much justification, at politicians who talked about their 'moral compass' but were either unwilling or unable to describe the direction in which it pointed. But critics of 'the vision thing' also targeted their scorn on social democrats who believed that Labour should be guided by a clear and coherent philosophy and argued that policy discussions should focus on the way in which the abiding principles could be applied to changing circumstances. New Labour advocated something which – although they called it modernization – amounted to fundamental change in Labour's core philosophy. The self-styled 'modernizers' argued that the principles which had guided Labour for a hundred years were irrelevant to the needs of Britain at the turn of the twentieth century. They wanted to replace belief in greater equality and the benefits of community action with the advocacy of meritocracy and the supposed advantages of individualism.

What passed for their philosophy of government was the Third Way – a rag-bag of half-thought-out ideas that defenders of the old verities claimed owed more to the opinion expressed in focus groups than any serious analysis of the country's problems and prospects. There is no doubt that New Labour – a clean break with the mistakes of the past – was, in part, created to improve the party's chances of ending the cycle of Conservative election victories. But that, in itself, is not an unworthy objective. And the men and women who were critical of the Third Way made a major strategic mistake by allowing the myth to grow that they preferred purity to power. Instead of moaning about the influence of opinion polls, they should have pointed to the incontrovertible evidence which confirmed that Labour did not have to choose between the two. In *Explaining Labour's Landslide,* Worcester and Mortimore leave no doubt that if, in 1997, the party had campaigned on a genuine social democratic manifesto, it would still have won the general election.[1] And the lesson that the Labour leadership should have learned from Margaret Thatcher was that the people admire politicians with firm and fixed principles – even when they do not agree with them.

Now Labour does have a choice. It can grub about in search of policies which will attract the swing voters and lose the next general election or it can become again an indisputable party of principle and win. Choosing the winning option does not mean a reversion to the policies of 1945 or 1964. The second strategic mistake made by the critics of the Third Way was the enthusiasm with which they accepted the title 'Old Labour'. After the defeat of 1979 the Labour Party had to change and more changes had to follow the three subsequent Conservative victories. But the debate that brought them about should have involved more than rival allegations of cynicism and sentimentality. During the ten years of office which followed, discussion of the future was always inhibited by fears of damaging the government. Now the acceptance of past mistakes is necessary to future success.

The architects of New Labour, sincerely believing that their ideas were right for the country, made several attempts to evolve a new 'centre left' philosophy. Communitarianism and triangulation preceded the Third Way – anything except 'old-fashioned' social democracy. And when they wrote and spoke about the importance of doing 'what works', there was the clear implication that the social democratic solution did not pass that test. All the variations of their theories were based on the simultaneously romantic and arrogant illusion that men and women of ability and integrity – unprejudiced by ideology – can come to an objective and generally accepted agreement about 'what is best for the whole community'. Indeed they held the view that philosophical preconceptions got in the way of good government. As a result, they joined the ranks of the 'practical men' who were identified by John Maynard Keynes as being 'slaves to some defunct economists'.

New Labour, and the ministers who shared its thinking, embraced the market – openly insisting that it was the automatic guarantee of economic efficiency and the best way of allocating resources. The government intervened to impose its will – as represented by 'targets' for hospitals and the threat of closure for schools – in the public sector. But it believed that the least government was the best government when decisions had to be made about influencing the conduct of private companies. What its proponents glorified as pragmatism looked like – and often was – inconsistency. Within the space of six months, plans to build a 'super-casino' in Manchester were scrapped – accompanied by admirable statements about the undesirability of encouraging gambling – and the law was changed to allow the opening of numerous local casinos and the television advertising of gambling – with equally robust statements about freedom of choice. In consequence of the *à la carte*, David Cameron felt able to ask Tony Blair at Prime Minister's Question Time, 'What is Labour for?' At one level the answer was obvious enough. Though it is right to notice that its undisputed successes – the national minimum wage, revitalized health service and record school building – were essentially 'Old Labour' while its acknowledged failures – the light-touch regulation of financial services and the private finance initiative – were 'New'. But because the party lacked an ethical framework on which to build its programme, Cameron's question resonated with uncommitted voters who sometimes too often believed that policies were being plucked out of the air or adopted to meet the demands of vested interests.

Richard Crossman wrote that Clement Attlee's Labour government 'has lost its way not only because it lacks a map of the new country it is crossing, but because it thinks maps unnecessary for experienced travellers'.[2] Exactly the same was true of the declining Blair and Brown years. The notion that decisions had to be related to an overriding principle was dismissed as old-fashioned and unrealistic. When Labour lost its way, its supporters lost heart.

Ed Miliband is now re-establishing its reputation – for moral and intellectual consistency – among an electorate which has lost faith in politics and politicians in general. He will not be successful in his endeavour to prove that Labour is a party of principle unless the party sets out clearly what its principles are. That process began at the 2012 party conference. I supported Ed Miliband during his Labour leadership campaign because he was the candidate of conviction and I believed that he would fight the general election in the same spirit. That belief was strengthened by his promise to build one nation. Whatever Benjamin Disraeli said during his speech in the Manchester Free Trade Hall, the subject of some discussion since Ed Miliband quoted from it, there is no doubt about Disraeli's views on the subject. They appear in his novel *Lothair* (1870). England, he wrote – meaning Britain – is 'two nations, the rich and poor'. And, in case his readers missed his message, he repeated it. In England 'the Privileged and the People form Two Nations'. Miliband's hope of uniting the divided country is an unashamed social democratic objective which can only be achieved by the promotion of social democracy's primary objective – the creation of a more equal society.

During his conference speech, Miliband also quoted a more conventional Labour authority – Clement Attlee, the prime minister who became a socialist because he 'did not like the kind of society we had and wanted something better'.[3] Attlee's ambition was not to win the class war, but to end it. That essentially moderate aspiration can only be realized by reducing the disparities between Disraeli's rich and poor. And that is not going to happen without the government actively promoting redistribution of power and wealth and an assault on those social barriers which divide the classes. Anyone who genuinely believes in 'One Nation' has to advocate the active pursuit of greater equality and accept that an interventionist government must play a major part in bringing it about. It is Ed Miliband's good fortune to lead the Labour Party at a time when its fundamental belief in greater equality, if properly explained, chimes with the national mood. And it is Labour's good fortune to be led by a politician who not only shares the beliefs on which the party was founded, but has enough confidence in both the strength of that idea and the wisdom of the British people to believe that Labour can win an election on its own, rather than on borrowed convictions.

Labour has always been reluctant to talk about what it has traditionally dismissed as 'theory'. For years it was argued that the needs were so great and the injustice so obvious that a programme of social reform did not need to be underpinned by a description of the philosophic idea on which it was based. That argument had some force when there was no health service and 2 million unemployed was accepted as the unavoidable consequences of what was called 'the trade cycle'. And the programme of the great Labour government of 1945 was so focused on the needs of the working classes that it processed the coherence of class-based politics. But the world has changed. It was much easier to argue the case for the establishment of free medical care, when none existed, than it is to insist that an increase in private provision within the health service will eventually undermine the basic principle of 'free at the point of use' – true though that is.

The old working class – as it existed and perceived itself 60 years ago – is no more. Now disadvantage and deprivation is more diffuse and, in consequence, less obvious. Even at the time that we were supposed 'never to have had it so good' there was a submerged percentage of the population who were badly housed and denied the education and health care that they needed. And now that the good days have gone, all the parties claim that they know the best way to guarantee their return. Labour has to demonstrate that its prescription is the one which works – for the whole country. That requires more than a collection of individual policy statements – no matter how radical and realistic they may be. It requires a clear statement of Labour's fundamental purpose – a task which the party has never accomplished with much distinction. The 1918 Constitution included the always contentious Clause Four – a declaration which Sydney Webb, its author, accepted was not to be taken seriously. Its replacement – said to be proof positive that Tony Blair had put his indelible stamp on the party – was, in terms of ideas, anodyne because it was incoherent.

Other Western European socialist and social democratic parties take it for granted that one of the objects of policy discussions is to decide how the abiding principles on which they are based can best be related to the realities of a fast changing world. The Labour Party – which shuffled off its association with the Marxist SDF as soon as it became a significant political force – has always feared that 'ideological speculation' would give the impression that it was working its way towards the 'dictatorship of the proletariat'. Harold Wilson used to *boast* that he had never read *Das Kapital.* The Blair government was obsessed with the need to prove that it was insulated from infiltration by the 'extremists' who had done the party so much damage in the early 1980s. In fact, Militant and its associated irritants were disposed of by the end of the decade. The infiltration of the 1990s came from the Right not the Left and the extremist influences were exerted by disciples of Hayek and Friedman not Lenin and Trotsky.

Perhaps, between the wars, G.D.H. Cole was right to argue that 'socialism almost without doctrines – so undefined in its doctrinal basis as to make recruits readily available among persons of quite different types' was the prescription for victory then, but not now.[4] Three years ago it left Labour with the blurred image which is fatal for political parties. Recovery has been achieved more quickly than it was reasonable to expect. That is because the case for social democracy is stronger now than it was – or has been perceived to be – for years. Social democrats have always argued that greater equality – as well as a moral imperative – would, by releasing neglected energy and talent, be of benefit to the whole community. Conversely, inequality – of power as well as wealth – damaged the long-term interests of every stratum of the community.

Social democracy's moment has come because the case for greater equality is now more widely accepted than it has ever been. That change in attitude is as much based on self-interest as on altruism. We know that there is a strong correlation between inequality and the social diseases which infect societies. The bigger the gap between rich and poor, the greater is the level of street crime, the more frequent are unwanted teenage pregnancies, the higher is the recorded level of drug addition, the more common is adult illiteracy with all the problems for employment that it creates. And we know too that increasing numbers of prosperous citizens regard living in the tranquillity of a stable society as more important than an annual increase in disposable income. 'Vote for equality and walk home safe at night' is perhaps not the advertising agencies' idea of an ideal slogan. But if Labour wants to fight the next election on the high moral ground – and at the same time say that its policies are down to earth – it is not a bad idea to feature this in the campaign.

It can stand shoulder to shoulder with the confident advocacy of that other essentially social democratic policy – the determination to use the power of the state to protect the community against the greed of the unscrupulous and often incompetent minority. Who now argues that 'light touch regulation' – based on the belief that banks were responsible, efficient and honest institutions – is the best way either to avoid another financial meltdown or to ensure that essential investment funds are available to companies with the potential for growth? Who now believes – following exposure of the neglect in care homes and the confirmation that cost-saving cuts in track maintenance was to blame for a major railway accident – that private enterprise can be trusted to own and manage those sectors of the economy in which people are more important than profits? Who now insists – as cuts in the provision of essential services prejudice the lives and health of the very old and very young – that local government is inherently wasteful, intrusive and authoritarian? Who now claims – as energy companies raise their tariffs when raw material prices rise, but fail to reduce them when they fall – that the public utilities are properly regulated? Who still demands – as the private sector stubbornly fails to create new jobs outside the golden south-east triangle and exports British jobs to low-wage economies – that government intervention in the economy is against the national interest?

The answer to all those questions is: those whose ideas are wilfully rooted in the past or who – because of ignorance or selfishness – turn their backs on the new reality. Over the next three years they will, in alliance with the defenders of social hierarchy and privilege, deploy all the old arguments against social democracy – outdated, extreme, ignorant and envious. Labour must face its critics head on. Principles are the way to power. The people want their politicians to do better than make a series of unrelated and often unrealizable promises. They want to hear of the better society which this country can become. It is time for 'the vision thing' – in the best and most intellectually coherent sense of that term – to find its way back into Labour politics.

NOTES

1. R. Worcester and R. Mortimore, *Explaining Labour's Landslide: How Tony Blair Swept to Victory*, London: Politicos, 1999
2. R.H.S. Crossman, 'Towards a Philosophy of Socialism' in R.H.S. Crossman (ed.) *New Fabian Essays*, London: Turnstile, 1952; p.2
3. C.A.R. Crosland, *The Future of Socialism*, London: Cape, 1956; p.116
4. Quoted in Crosland, *The Future of Socialism*, p.80

INTRODUCTION

Kevin Hickson and Pete Redford

THE CASE FOR SOCIALISM IN MODERN BRITAIN

The aim of this book is a bold one: to demonstrate that socialism (or social democracy) is the right path for the Labour Party: morally, economically and politically. It does so in the belief that not only is socialism the way to a fairer society – more equal and more just – but also to an efficient and stable economy.

The tone of the book is decidedly optimistic. This may seem a little out of place. Times are difficult and there are very real constraints on what a future Labour government can do given the lack of economic growth and the state of the public finances. However, this is also a time to be more optimistic about what can be achieved.

Firstly, because neo-liberal, free market capitalism has proven in a very spectacular way that it no longer works, if indeed it ever did, there is a profound sense of unease that those who did most to cause the banking crisis and subsequent recession have got away with it. Although some may wish to describe this as 'envy', it is more accurate to understand this sentiment as a deep sense of social injustice. If elected politicians do not seek to reflect that sense of unease in their policies then there is a tendency for it to erupt into direct action as seen on the streets of our major cities in 2011. An equally undesirable outcome is the identification of scapegoats: classic right-wing moral panics encapsulated by the pervasiveness of terms such as 'broken society' which seek to blame the ills of society on the 'work-shy', 'feckless' or the 'underclass'.

In the 'good society' which everyone on the Left wishes to see, everyone has rights but also responsibilities to each other. Predictably those on the Right argued that responsibilities were only the concern of the poor, where a distinction between the deserving and undeserving emerged during the Thatcher and Major years. Regrettably, this attitude persisted during the New Labour years. It has become an unfortunate fact of modern society that the most vulnerable are criticized by populist politicians and journalists, often in ignorance of the facts. There was no corresponding emphasis on the responsibilities of the rich, no distinction between a 'deserving' and 'undeserving' rich. The idea that responsibilities correspond with rights all the way up is at the heart of Ed Miliband's call for One Nation.[1] If One Nation does not mean a reduction in the gap between the rich and the poor then it means nothing at all. Miliband has put the issue of equality back at the heart of Labour Party thinking where it belongs.

But inequality is not just wrong socially, it is also wrong economically. The promise of quick returns and the belief that profit maximization should be the sole objective of privately owned corporations has been deeply damaging to our long-term economic success. This is what Ed Miliband meant when he boldly critiqued 'predatory capitalism'.[2] Instead we should be seeking to emulate the best features of German and Scandinavian models of capitalism, with the emphasis of the former on long-termism, planning and partnership, while equality and welfare are features associated with the latter. It is striking that these countries have survived the banking crisis of 2007–8 much more resiliently than Britain and the United States which were overly reliant on their banking sectors after several years of neo-liberal economic orthodoxy. It is quite clear that not all countries were hit equally hard by the 'global financial crisis'.

Democratic socialists should therefore have confidence in their ideology, not just socially but also economically. Having confidence also means believing that it is the right thing to do politically. Being explicit in our ideological commitment is the best, if not the only way to secure power at the next general election. It means accepting that although the New Labour electoral strategy worked amazingly well in the context of the mid-1990s it is not relevant in the very different circumstances of today. Labour, or 'New Labour', lost 5 million votes between 1997 and 2010. Of these many went to what were perceived as alternative left-wing parties such as the Greens, Plaid Cymru, SNP, SDLP and the Liberal Democrats. More went to the Conservatives, presumably believing that the party had changed under Cameron. Worryingly, the party also lost support to more right-wing parties such as the BNP and UKIP. Strikingly, around one and a half million abstained. There was a feeling in Labour's heartlands that the party had abandoned many of its traditional supporters. That it hadn't made much difference to the lives of ordinary people and had failed. This is not justified in the sense that the last Labour government did progress towards a fairer society. However, it all too often failed to champion its social democratic successes. To do so risked looking like 'old fashioned' leftists.

In order to win the next general election, Labour must appeal to a broad section of the electorate in many different parts of the country. Concentrating on an artificial 'median voter' or stressing the apparent concerns of southern voters above others will not work. The only way to win is to have confidence in our ideology in order to encourage people to vote positively for Labour. If the Labour Party is to mount an effective electoral strategy it cannot do so without the engagement of local members, yet again if it cannot offer a clear vision of what it wants to do in power then it is not going to enlist their active support. This calls for a very different strategy than has been the norm in British politics since the mid-1990s. It means abandoning the core/periphery distinction in the realization that it is in many once safe Labour areas that turnout has been a very real issue. Labour needs to have a strategy which can appeal to core and floating voters alike and the only way it can do this is to espouse the kind of values it wishes to see implemented if it is fortunate enough to win the next general election. Labour must develop a language which speaks for the majority. Once again, Ed Miliband has done this with his emphasis on the 'squeezed middle'. Although this idea was ridiculed it has resonated with the electorate and has become a standard phrase among journalists.[3]

It also means refocusing on the importance of an active central state. Unfortunately recent contributions to the political thought of the Labour Party have tended to embrace the critique of the central state mounted by David Cameron in his vision of the Big Society. Localism is in vogue. Yet localism offers very little to the major issues of the day. If you want to have effective regulation of the banking sector you need active government. If you want to restore economic growth you need the government to intervene. If you wish to resolve the major social or ecological issues which confront us nations need to work together. The reason why people are critical of the state is because it hasn't done enough to confront the problems of our age.

There has been too little state intervention, not too much. To leave people to the whim of the market or tell them to solve problems in their local communities is to leave them without a countervailing power to the overwhelming forces of capitalism. None of this means embracing the unreformed state. There is still plenty to do in terms of reconnecting people with the state and to restore trust in politicians and the political process. But without the state, social democracy is hollowed out and the creation of a just society is an impossible dream.

Nor does a focus on the nation state mean that we are isolationist. There is a need to develop a new approach to foreign policy which allows for the fostering of a genuine internationalism and humanitarianism, and which respects the role of international institutions such as the United Nations. If we are not to lapse into a dangerous form of national rivalry, we need to remake the case for Europe. If we are to avoid environmental disaster we need to work collectively. Other problems such as terrorism and crime no longer stop at national borders. Socialism is inherently an internationalist creed, which is why even some friends of the Labour Party are wrong to suggest we should try to turn back the clock and withdraw into isolationism.

The rationale for this book, therefore, is to remake the case for democratic socialism or social democracy (we use these terms interchangeably). Since it offers the only real answers to the major issues of the day it is socialism that is the most appropriate basis for the Labour Party as it moves towards the next general election and beyond. Socialism, properly understood, combines the right principles with sensible policies.

THE STRUCTURE OF THE BOOK

The book is divided into five main sections. The first section deals with economic policy. Considerable focus is given to economic policy, broadly understood, since it is in the economic sphere that neo-liberalism has most obviously failed. William Keegan analyses the immediate economic context and remakes the case for Keynesian social democracy. Keynesianism is said to have failed in 1976 with the IMF crisis, but made a brief return in response to the banking crisis. Keegan argues that Gordon Brown's response was essentially correct and argues that Keynesianism is a far more satisfactory policy now than the austerity agenda of the Coalition. Stewart Lansley then sets out the case for wider, longer-term structural reform of the economy based on greater equality. Specific aspects of the economy are then discussed. Bill Kerry makes the argument for more mixed forms of corporate ownership including mutuals and renationalization. Michael Meacher examines environmental policy, having been a long-standing authority on this subject. Finally, David Coats explores the issue of industrial democracy and highlights its contemporary significance. Overall, what these chapters show is that an alternative to neo-liberalism is not only desirable but also feasible.

Going on to examine what a socialist society would look like, Ruth Lister remakes the argument for equality, understood as more than just equality of opportunity and encompassing a concern with outcomes. In the following two chapters members of Labour's front bench outline the evolving approach in two key policy areas. Lisa Nandy sets out the thinking on education and young people and Andy Burnham articulates a 'whole-person' approach to health and social care policy. Not only do these two chapters demonstrate what is wrong with Coalition policy but they also flesh out a more positive agenda, emphasizing the role of the state at both national and local levels. Finally in this section of the book Raymond Plant and Robert Page discuss how socialist principles can be applied to public service reform and the welfare state in the twenty-first century. Once again, these chapters show the way to a radically different approach to neo-liberalism, with policy designed to achieve clearly articulated socialist values.

Several chapters discuss the role of the state under a democratic socialist framework. David Walker remakes the case for 'centralism' against the current fashion of localism. David Moon seeks to re-establish the case for the Union against the rise of nationalism in Wales and Scotland. It is crucial if Labour wants to remain the party of the Union, and therefore a viable electoral force in British politics, that it starts to make a positive case for Scotland remaining in the Union. Simon Slater makes the argument for empowering local government, believing that only the return of greater powers – and not pursuing structural reform such as elected mayors – is the way to revive local democracy. Andrew Vincent then explores the social democratic philosophy of the state. Finally, Helena Kennedy argues passionately for the central importance of civil liberties as part of a democratic socialist strategy and reflects critically on the New Labour era.

The next section discusses socialist internationalism. Peter Kilfoyle seeks to revive the idea of an ethical foreign policy first articulated by Robin Cook after the 1997 general election defeat. Peter Hain then sets out further what a progressive internationalist agenda would look like. Finally in this section, Arlene McCarthy discusses the ways in which the case for European integration can be remade in the face of the current eurozone crisis.

Having discussed the major areas of policy, the final section of the book examines the political and electoral strategy for socialism. Paul Hunter sets out a detailed psephological examination of voting trends since 1997 and concludes that such an analysis suggests that Labour needs to be more ideological if it is to win the next general election. An accommodation to the 'middle ground' along the lines of New Labour's electoral strategy will not work in the very different conditions of 2014–15 than 1997. The final three chapters offer perspectives on how this may be achieved. Helen Goodman demonstrates, with some practical examples, how the language of socialism needs to be relevant to people's needs if it is to resonate with them. John Denham outlines the case for 'progressive patriotism' advanced by Ed Miliband with his One Nation speech at the 2012 Labour Party Conference. Both Goodman and Denham argue that the most effective way to reconnect voters with socialist principles is to ground them in the language of the community and the everyday experience of citizens. We should avoid speaking in abstract terms. The concluding chapter, from Andrew Harrop, shows the enduring appeal of Labour's traditional values.

The authors all share the broad thesis that is set out in this Introduction, although disagreement remains on specific issues. This is not only understandable but to be encouraged as part of the discussion on the future of the Labour Party. There is broad agreement over the ends, but valid disagreement over the means of a socialist strategy. Not all policy areas can or have been covered in this book. There will no doubt be some contemporary issues and aspects of public policy which some readers may have wished to have seen included. It is not that we do not feel that socialism can talk to these issues and policy areas, but rather the lack of space in a book that has already grown in size. We sincerely hope that this book continues the dialogue and debate that was initiated by the publication of the editors' 'In Praise of Social Democracy' in *The Political Quarterly* in the belief that it is essential to a Labour victory.[4]

****

There are many people who the editors would like to thank for their contribution to this book, not least the authors themselves. They all have busy lives and many competing demands on their time and so we are very grateful for their involvement. We have been fortunate to have such an intellectually distinguished team. Our publisher I.B.Tauris – especially our commissioning editor, Jo Godfrey – has been very supportive throughout.

Kevin Hickson would like to give a special word of thanks to several people in particular. The first is to Pete Redford for both his substantial intellectual and practical contribution to this project. Second, to David Moon who has been a source of encouragement and reassurance throughout the editing of this book even as he wrote his own excellent chapter. Matt and Claire Beech have listened patiently to me as I talked endlessly about this project. Last, but certainly by no means least, Maggie Pearlstine for her advice and encouragement along the way.

NOTES

1. Ed Miliband, speech to the Labour Party Conference, 2 October 2012
2. Ed Miliband, speech to the Labour Party Conference, 26 September 2011
3. See, for instance, S. Malik, 'Lexicographers cram "squeezed middle" into word of the year slot', *Guardian*, 23 November 2011, www.guardian.co.uk/books/2011/nov/23/squeezed-middle-word-of-year
4. R. Hattersley and K. Hickson, 'In Praise of Social Democracy', *The Political Quarterly*, 83/1, 2012, pp. 5–12

PART I

A SOCIAL DEMOCRATIC ECONOMY

Chapter 1

KEYNES VERSUS HOUSEHOLD ECONOMICS

William Keegan

THATCHERISM RIDES AGAIN

That this book is needed at all demonstrates just how difficult it is to get the fundamental Keynesian message across. Almost everywhere I go I encounter some version of Mrs Thatcher's 'household economics'. According to this school, when private citizens and businesses are 'cutting back' then it is incumbent on government to do the same.

A typical example of this thinking, which is all too prevalent, was contained in an article by the Chief Executive of Tesco in the *Financial Times* on 19 September 2012. 'Families across Britain are trying to live within their means,' Mr Philip Clarke wrote, 'the Coalition government must do the same...The most important question of our time is how government can improve people's lives without simply borrowing more money.'[1]

The answer is that government cannot meet Mr Clarke's request without borrowing more money. There is, to coin a phrase, no alternative. The only way to emerge from recession is for the government to induce an increase in what economists call 'aggregate demand' – the sum total of all goods and services purchased in the economy. An important rider, of course, is that it is not much help if all the extra money goes on imports: there must be a reasonable balance in a nation's trading position.

If the private sector is cutting back, then cuts in public spending, or higher taxes, only compound the problem. What the government needs to do is to borrow its way out of recession until it restores the economy to a decent rate of growth. All experience shows that when the economy is expanding at its full potential, then the budgetary position improves rapidly, as happened, for instance, in the spurt of growth under the chancellorship of Kenneth Clarke which followed the Black Wednesday debacle of 1992.

The whole point about an enlightened economic policy is that, in the face of prolonged depression, a government can take a longer view of what it is to 'live within one's means'. With unemployment so high, and so much unused capacity in industry and the service economy, a boost to demand is required – a boost that will automatically increase the tax base and reduce concerns about the budget deficit.

Time and time again over the years the Conservatives have brought up the conference speech made by Jim Callaghan in 1976, when he said a government could no longer spend its way out of recession. But that passage was inserted entirely for tactical purposes, to pacify the International Monetary Fund and a US Treasury dominated at the time by extreme right-wingers, in the shape of Secretary William Simon and his deputy Ed Yeo. Callaghan later repudiated that point, and made clear, in his memoirs *Time and Chance*, his opposition to the deflationary policies of the first, 1979–83, Thatcher government.[2]

Those were years when 'Keynesianism' had run into trouble, as successive governments became overambitious with their expansionary policies, encountering formidable wage inflation, which had been given a hefty push by the impact of the oil crises of the 1970s, and the ill-timed indexation of wages to prices.

Although often they were merely trying to protect their members from an erosion of their living standards, the trades unions were generally considered to be the culprits behind the wage/price/wage spiral which obsessed politicians, officials and economists during what one might call the pre-Thatcher period.

But if there is one thing that the combination of Mrs Thatcher's assault on the unions and the ultra-competitive forces of the 'globalization' of the labour force has achieved, it is the humbling of the unions. The current policy of 'expansionary fiscal contraction' adopted by the Coalition takes place against an altogether different background from previous postwar deflationary episodes.

THE AUSTRIAN SCHOOL REOPENED

That background, of course, is the financial crisis of 2007–8, the repercussions of which are very much still with us. The crisis has led to a revival of an earlier debate between the Keynesians and what is sometimes referred to as 'the Austrian school', although my Austrian friends such as Dr Hannes Androsch, who was finance minister of his country when Denis Healey was chancellor here, point out that not all Austrians belong to that school.

What school, since you ask? Well, it is the school of thinking that believes there are historic phases when an economy needs to be 'purged'. Joseph Schumpeter, that well-known Austrian economist, sang the praises of the 'creative destruction' of capitalism. And the classical school of economists believed in the ultimately self-righting properties of markets. Keynes, on the other hand, argued that economies could remain depressed for a very long time after a shock of the sort experienced in 2007–8, unless governments took corrective action.

The distinguished economist Lionel Robbins was for a time close to the Austrian school. As John Eatwell and Murray Milgate point out in their book *The Fall and Rise of Keynesian Economics*: 'if markets really were mechanisms that could be relied upon to allocate scarce resources in the most efficient manner, as Lionel Robbins had incautiously proclaimed in the middle of the Great Depression, then persistent and sustained underutilisation of those resources would be a virtual impossibility.'[3] Yet there was mass involuntary unemployment and massive unused industrial capacity in front of everyone's eyes.

I got to know Lord Robbins when I was Economics Correspondent of the *Financial Times* in the late 1960s and early 1970s, and he was chairman. He was the most delightful, unassuming man, and readily conceded that on this issue he had been wrong and Keynes was right in the debates of the 1930s – although he always thought Keynes was wrong to favour controls on imports at one stage.

However, there is a terrible irony about the title of the Eatwell/Milgate book. It was being worked on at a time when, thanks not least to the missionary efforts of Prime Minister Gordon Brown, there was a concerted Keynesian approach to the 2007–8 financial crisis, culminating in the successful G20 summit in London on 1–2 April 2009.

SAVING THE WORLD?

That was the period when, in Gordon Brown's Freudian slip in the House of Commons, our then prime minister 'saved the world'. In fact that phrase was used for the (almost) concerted operation on both sides of the Atlantic to re-capitalize the banking system, in the summer of 2008. The 'Keynesian' agreement, under the auspices of the G20, to inject a massive $1 trillion stimulus into the ailing world economy was made at that G20 summit in London, after much hard work by Gordon Brown. Brown happened, while under fire at home for his lacklustre domestic premiership, to be the right man, in the right place, at the right time, both in autumn 2008 and spring 2009, to manifest seriously impressive international leadership, winning praise from everyone from Barack Obama to President Sarkozy, and even *Time* magazine.

It seemed indeed like the rise of Keynesian economics; but the celebrations were short-lived. In May 2010 Brown was ousted from power, at a time when, thanks to the sensible toleration of a growing budget deficit caused largely by the financial crisis, and the stimulus of a reduction in VAT and specific measures to assist the car industry, the British economy was manifestly emerging, albeit slowly, from recession.

We then experienced something pretty close to a laboratory experiment, under which the incoming chancellor, George Osborne, in a fit of culpable misjudgement, misleadingly compared the British economic predicament to that of Greece. This was at a time when Greece appeared to be weeks away from running out of money, whereas the average maturity on Britain's public debt was some 14 years.

The announcement of the austerity programme was enough to stop the burgeoning recovery in its tracks; and the premature increase in VAT completed the business. After that came the succession of budget cuts, hitting both the public sector and private sector contractors who depend on public sector orders – cuts which, as I write in October 2012, are due to mount in severity.

The Osborne strategy, now a manifest failure for all to see, was the consequence of one of the most cynical political calculations I have witnessed in decades of reporting and commenting on the British economy.

THE BLAME GAME

What the incoming chancellor decided to do was exaggerate the scale of the deficit problem; blame it all on Labour, as if the Conservatives had not supported the previous government's public spending plans at the time; and talk as if the deficit had nothing to do with the financial crisis. He would go hell for leather to eliminate the so-called 'structural deficit' over the course of the Parliament; stabilize and bring down the debt to GDP ratio; and engineer an impressive pre-election recovery. (The 'structural' deficit is that element of the budget deficit which is putatively not attributable to purely 'cyclical' factors. It is not that easy to measure or distinguish, and can easily be exaggerated. Experience shows that it is surprising how, during a period of rapid 'cyclical' growth, a 'structural' deficit can evaporate.)

The Coalition claimed to have the support of the Bank of England, but the Bank of England is not infallible. There is no doubt that, although Sir Mervyn King has conceded that the timing and size of the budget cuts can be open to debate, he is generally seen to have bestowed his blessing right from the start, on the broad strategy of deficit reduction, although he is understood to object to suggestions that he secretly 'read the riot act' to Osborne and Clegg on the subject. The Bank's line is that the Governor said nothing of substance to the Coalition leaders that he had not said publicly.

More recently, as the 'reduction' strategy has run into trouble – as predicted, most notably by Shadow Chancellor Ed Balls – King has made a point of saying that there can be some leeway. Sir Mervyn is a respected academic economist. But so is Professor Larry Summers of Harvard, who has written several impressive articles in the *Financial Times*, pointing to the self-defeating nature of deficit reduction at a time of such high unemployment and such low use of industrial capacity.

Clearly, once normality is restored – and the government's response to the crisis has probably delayed such a development – there should be strict budgetary discipline and the current budget deficit should be brought back under control. But at the time of writing we are nowhere near that point.

Before becoming Deputy Governor and then Governor, Sir Mervyn King was the Bank of England's Chief Economist. One of his distinguished predecessors was Christopher Dow, whose last book *Major Recessions* went into great historical detail about the causes and consequences of recessions.[4] One of Dow's key findings was that, in contrast to the Coalition/Bank of England current reliance on monetary policy, fiscal expansion over a period of years was necessary if the economy was to emerge from a major recession.

GETTING OUT OF THE HOLE

Denis Healey (chancellor 1974–9) used to say: 'if you are in a hole, don't dig deeper'. Yet that is precisely what Chancellor Osborne has done. Blaming it on the eurozone will not do. The return to recession – I prefer, with the National Institute of Economic and Social Research to regard it as a *depression* – was begun in Downing Street, even though some of the key influences depressing consumer spending, such as the higher oil price, were not.

Where Osborne is especially culpable is in the way that he has managed to encourage the 'anti' Keynesians around the world in the process. False analogies have been made with the fiscal contraction experienced in Canada in the 1990s, with claims that the Canadian recovery proves that 'fiscal contraction' was indeed expansionary. Closer examination, however, shows that the Canadian recovery of that decade was already well under way, with world trade and US/Canadian cross-border trade booming, before the fiscal squeeze was introduced.

The idea that future generations will somehow suffer if there is not drastic action now to eliminate the deficit is risible. Future generations are more likely to suffer from the delayed consequences of cuts in public sector investment. As Professor Summers and others, including Martin Wolf of the *Financial Times*, have pointed out, the government ought to be taking advantage of negligible interest rates to invest in all manner of public sector investment which would benefit future generations as well as providing work for the present generation.

There is also a way in which the government could combine Keynesian reflationary policies with an attempt to redress the gulf between rich and poor which is now concerning even Ferdinand Mount, a former head of Mrs Thatcher's policy unit.[5] That is to concentrate a boost to spending power – effective demand, in Keynesian parlance – on the poor, who are more likely to spend than to save.

It is time to combat the almost masochistic public mood which demands that everyone must cut back. It is a tragedy that the nation is having to relearn the Keynesian insight that expenditure cuts and tax increases weaken output and employment and can have a perverse effect on the budget deficit they are designed to reduce.

It would also be a tragedy if Labour continued heading for the trap in which they define themselves in macro-economic terms as a party that would cut like the Coalition, but more slowly. Cuts during a continued depression, or illusory recovery, are economically and socially harmful; they are also likely to be self-defeating. The time for cuts is when the economy is restored to health. At the time of writing (October 2012) that time is far distant, and will be even more distant if governments persist with a pre-Keynesian 'strategy' of 'expansionary fiscal contraction'.

NOTES

1. P. Clarke, 'Lessons in Store for Austerity Britain', *Financial Times*, 19 September 2012

2. J. Callaghan, *Time and Chance*, London: Collins, 1987

3. J. Eatwell and M. Milgate, *The Fall and Rise of Keynesian Economics*, New York: Oxford University Press, 2011; p.3

4. C. Dow, *Major Recessions: Britain and the World, 1920–95*, Oxford: Oxford University Press, 1998

5. F. Mount, *The New Few or A Very British Oligarchy: Power and Inequality in Britain Now*, London: Simon and Schuster, 2012

Chapter 2

EQUALITY AND ECONOMIC STABILITY

Stewart Lansley

Over the last 60 years, social democracy in the UK has moved from ascendancy in the postwar era to marginalization from the early 1980s and then to 'the Third Way' period of accommodation to markets from the mid-1990s.

A key element of this accommodation was the scaling back of a fundamental Labour principle, a belief in a more equal society. It was this commitment that helped drive the postwar narrowing of the wealth and income gap, a process which came to a halt during the global crisis of the 1970s and then went sharply into reverse. Today, the income gap has returned to a level last seen in the 1930s. This reversal has been driven by a new economic philosophy, one that argued that egalitarianism had gone too far, that a sharp dose of inequality and bigger rewards at the top would kick-start enterprise and boost growth.

This new thinking emerged from two influential strands of thought. First, from a group of New Right, pro-market thinkers such as the Austrian-American economist Ludwig von Mises. As he put it in 1955: 'inequality of wealth and incomes is the cause of the masses' well being, not the cause of anybody's distress...Where there is a lower degree of inequality, there is necessarily a lower standard of living of the masses.'[1] It was a view echoed by Sir Keith Joseph, one of Mrs Thatcher's most trusted advisers, in 1976. 'Making the rich poorer does not make the poor richer...The pursuit of income equality will turn this country into a totalitarian slum.'[2]

It was a theory – for theory it was – that gained further backing from a separate stream of economic thinking, one first outlined in an influential book, *Equality and Efficiency: The Big Tradeoff*, by the leading American economist Arthur Okun, published in 1975. Okun argued that you could have a more equal society or a more efficient one, but not both.[3]

From the beginning of the 1980s, the anti-egalitarian school achieved a degree of political dominance once held by the founding fathers of social democracy. Among those captured by the new creed was the New Labour leadership. As shown in Ruth Lister's chapter (this volume), Tony Blair favoured equality of opportunity over equality of outcome. He argued that he had 'no time for the politics of envy' and that it didn't matter how much the rich earned. Stephen Byers, trade secretary from December 1998, said that wealth creation was now more important than wealth distribution.

New Labour embraced the idea that too much equality would be a drag on economic progress. As long as tackling poverty was made a priority, then the rich should be allowed to flourish. The accumulation of large fortunes might bring a bigger divide, but by encouraging business, job and wealth creation would eventually make everybody better off through an expanded economic cake. It was the widespread acceptance of soaring levels of personal wealth, and the growing polarization that went with it, that became one of the defining characteristics of the shift away from the social democratic values that had once dominated postwar politics and opinion.

Between 1997 and 2010, the income gap between the top and the rest continued its upward trend with the gains from growth becoming increasingly colonized by big business and a small group of financiers, bankers and business executives. From 2000 to 2007, median chief executive pay rose six times faster than median earnings. Over the same period, the top 1% of earners increased their share of the economic pie by close to three percentage points.

So has the experiment in greater inequality delivered on the promise of greater economic success? The answer is no. The wealth gap has soared but without the promised pay-off of wider economic progress. On all measures of economic performance bar inflation, the post-1980 era of rising inequality has a much poorer record than the egalitarian postwar decades.

Since 1980 the UK economy has experienced slower growth and a more sluggish rise in productivity, while unemployment has been running at more than three times the average of the two postwar decades.[4] This is despite a steady fall in the share of national output accruing to wage-earners, from around 60% at the end of the 1970s to 53% by 2008, a trend that was meant to unleash a new era of record job creation. Financial crises have also become much more frequent and more damaging. As shown in Figure 1, the three post-1980 recessions have been much deeper and longer than those of the 1950s and 1960s, culminating in the crisis of the last four years.

The main outcome of the post-1980 experiment has been an economy that is both much more polarized *and* much more prone to crisis. So what does this tell us about cause and effect? Has the rise in inequality contributed to more fragile and unstable economies, making it a key factor in the 2008 crash and the persistence of the current crisis? History certainly shows a clear link *from* inequality *to* instability. The two most damaging crashes of the last century – 1929 and 2008 – were both *preceded* by sharp rises in inequality.

The mechanism by which excessive concentrations of income trigger economic malfunction is embedded in changes in the relationship between wages and productivity, a key link in the way economies function. If they get out of line in either direction, imbalances are created that lead to economic failure.

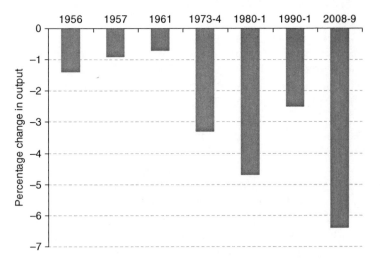

Figure 1   The record on recessions. *Source:* Lansley, *The Cost of Inequality*, p.132

Over the last century, this relationship has followed three separate patterns. For the two and a half decades from the end of the Second World War, wages and productivity moved broadly in line across richer nations. The proceeds of rising prosperity were evenly shared. This was also a period of relative economic stability. Next, for a brief period from the early 1970s, wages rose more quickly than productivity across the globe, a period that became known as the 'profits squeeze'. This was a time of deep economic crisis and stagflation.

Then there have been two periods when wages have lagged productivity – in the 1920s and the post-1980s – both periods culminating in deep-seated and prolonged slumps. Figure 2 shows that between 1990 and 2007 real wages in the UK rose more slowly than productivity and at an accelerating rate. In the United States, the decoupling started earlier and has led to an even larger gap. A number of other countries have seen a similar, if shallower, gap.

There are three key reasons why a growing 'wage–productivity gap' upsets the natural mechanisms necessary to achieve economic stability. First, de-linking earnings and output sucks demand out of economies and imposes deflation. In most rich economies, wage-enabled consumption accounts for around two-thirds of economic demand. If the wage pool falls substantially below this level, as in the

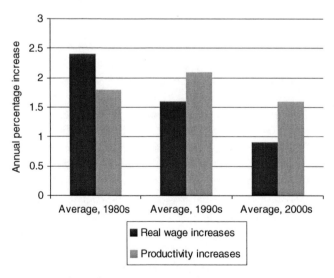

Figure 2   The UK's growing wage–productivity gap, 1980 to 2008.
Source: Lansley, *The Cost of Inequality*, p.50

1920s and the two decades to 2008, purchasing power falls behind the extra output being produced. Consumer societies suddenly find they lack the capacity to consume.

Without counteracting policies that lift demand, economies would seize up. In both the 1920s and the post-1990s, the demand gap was filled by an explosion of private debt. Personal debt rose three-and-a-half times faster than national income in the UK in the 25 years to 2008. Without this stimulus to demand, a deep-seated recession would have occurred much earlier. But pumping in private debt didn't prevent recession, it merely delayed it.

Second, concentrating the proceeds of growth in the hands of a small global financial elite eventually leads to asset bubbles. In 1920s America, enrichment at the top merely fed years of specula-tive activity in property and the stock market. The build-up to 2008 followed a near identical pattern. From the early 1990s, rising corpo-rate surpluses, uncontrolled bank lending and burgeoning personal wealth led to a giant mountain of global footloose capital. By 2008, the assets – loans, credit advances and derivatives – held by the ten largest UK banks had grown to nearly five times the size of the UK economy. The cash sums held by the world's global rich doubled in the decade to 2008 to a massive $39 trillion, a sum equivalent to slightly more than three times the size of the annual output of the American economy.

Far from creating new wealth, a tsunami of hot money raced around the world at speed in search of faster and faster returns, creating the bubbles – in property, commodities and business – that eventually brought the American, British and global economies to their knees.

Third, the traditional role of finance capitalism – to create wealth through productive investment – became increasingly sidelined. This is because the growing rewards that emerged in finance greatly distorted business incentives. Far from working to grow the size of the pie, the much expanded finance sector engaged in a battle to grab a larger share of it. Billions poured into takeovers, private equity, property and financial and industrial engineering. These delivered ever-higher fees and fortunes for the 'marriage brokers' construct-ing the deals, but increasingly via the transfer of existing rather than the much more difficult and risky task of creating new businesses, wealth and jobs from scratch.

In the decade to 2007, while bank lending for property develop-ment and takeover activity surged, the share going to manufacturing shrank by more than half to settle at a mere 2.4%. Britain's sustained boom from the late 1990s was a myth. While the contribution to the economy made by financial services more than doubled over this period, manufacturing shrank by one-quarter. During the UK's boom years, the money and productive sectors of the economy were moving in opposite directions.

New Labour's leaders were right in arguing that the Left needs to have a more coherent policy for wealth creation. That is the route to wider prosperity for all. But the evidence of the last 30 years is that a widening income gap and a more productive economy do not go hand in hand. What has been built is an increasingly wealth-diverting model of capitalism.

It is now being more widely accepted that excessive levels of inequality end in lower growth and greater instability. As one study of the efficiency/inequality trade-off by two IMF economists, Andrew Berg and Jonathan Ostry, has concluded: 'when growth is looked at over the long term, the (*efficiency/inequality*) trade-off may not exist. In fact equality appears to be an important ingredient in promoting and sustaining growth.'[5]

In addition, there is evidence that these macro-economic arguments are supported at the level of the firm. A number of academic studies – covering large and small firms in both North America and Europe – have shown a strong correlation between narrower pay dispersion within an organization and improved organization performance.[6] This research suggests that wide gaps between top and bottom pay harms performance overall.

Despite this, the best evidence is that inequality has continued to grow through the crisis. In the US, 93% of all income growth in 2010 went to the wealthiest 1%.[7] In the UK, real wages fell on average by 7% in the two years from the end of 2009 while the income gap between top and bottom continued to widen. Figure 3 compares the course of top executive (for FTSE 100 companies) remuneration with median full-time earnings since 2000. Not only did executive pay greatly outstrip average earnings growth up to 2007, apart from a slight blip in 2009 it has continued to do so.

The architects of the 'Third Way' era were wrong to sign up to the orthodoxy that economic dynamism could be achieved by greater inequality and the empowerment of finance. New Labour in office were also mistaken to leave the burden of creating a fairer society to a restructured system of income support. The case for a smaller income gap, traditionally based on social justice and fairness, now

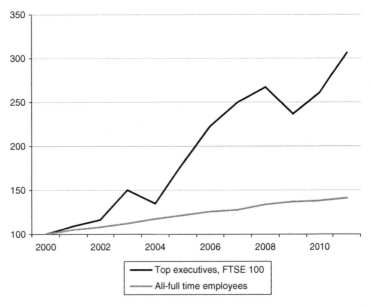

Figure 3   Index of top executive and employee pay, 2000–11 (in thousands of
pounds p.a.). *Source:* Income Data Services

needs to be extended to embrace the evidence about the damaging
economic impact of more polarized economies. A model of capitalism that fails to share the proceeds of growth more proportionately
is not sustainable.

It is not just social democrat thinkers who have warned of the
dangers of the excessive concentration of wealth and power on the
way economies function. 'All for ourselves and nothing for other
people', warned Adam Smith, the founding father of market economics, in *The Wealth of Nations*, 'seems, in every age of the world,
to have been the vile maxim of the masters of mankind.'[8]

Of course, a renewed commitment to a more equal society is one
thing. Delivering it is quite another. After a sustained and deeply
embedded process of reverse equalization, narrowing the gap would
require radical change on a number of fronts. Redistribution remains
important, but is only part of the solution. Equally vital is a more progressive tax system and much tougher action on tax havens, so that
more of the cost of income support is borne by the highly paid and
the very rich. At the moment, too much of the cost of welfare support
falls on those on middle incomes. A much greater emphasis also needs

to be placed on tackling inequality at source, by edging up the wage share and narrowing the pay gap. This means sharing the outcomes of markets more evenly before the application of tax/benefit measures.

Achieving a more equal 'pre-distribution' of incomes requires steering the economy in the direction of a very different model of capitalism, one closer to the continental than the US model and one which embraces a much greater sense of corporate responsibility, while downgrading the excessively dominant role played by the chase for shareholder value. It means achieving a much more even spread of power across the economy and society, wrenching it away from the modern-day equivalents of 'the masters of mankind' – big business, the financial sector and their lobbyists – in favour of manufacturing, traditional entrepreneurialism, customers and the workforce. This means tougher regulation, a very different and more focused role for finance and the strengthening of the role of collective bargaining.

It also requires a quite different set of social norms, with a less tolerant attitude to excess, more transparency in pay-setting and an end to the sense of entitlement that continues to prevail in the City and Wall Street. Such norms were highly relevant to the culture of restraint at the top that acted to cap rewards in the immediate postwar era.

Also needed is a new approach to economic management, one which elevates the pursuit of a more equal society to a primary goal of domestic and global economic policy and which integrates it into wider macroeconomic policy. This would mean a largely enhanced role for the state, one that extends intervention beyond redistribution and welfarism for securing a more even distribution of income and wealth.

In the UK since the 1980s, the role and impact of inequality has played at best a marginal role in economic management under governments of all political colours. Although there were plenty of debates at the highest levels about social mobility and tackling poverty during the post-1997 Labour years, the wider question of the division of factor shares and the macroeconomic impact of changes in the concentration of income were more or less completely ignored.

No single economic forecasting model in the UK incorporates the impact of changes in the distribution of income on vital outcomes like private investment, consumption, living standards, overall demand in the economy and key asset prices. This is all the more significant in that the Office for Budget Responsibility has predicted that labour's share of output will fall by more than a further three percentage points between 2009 and 2015.

The question of 'factor distribution' ought to be a key issue in strategic economic thinking. This determines the course of average living standards and has a major impact on economic stability and durability. Yet it slips through the net of current policy making machinery. The government needs to add a new set of economic indicators – including pay ratios, the wage share and the concentration of income at the top – to those of inflation, productivity, growth and unemployment.

Each indicator should be given a target that is compatible with economic stability. Thus the wage-share target should be set at the average of the two postwar decades – 59% – a level that brought equilibrium and sustained stability. It is currently well below target. Average tax rates should rise by income decile. At the moment, they are higher amongst lower- than higher-income households. The share of income enjoyed by the top 1% currently stands at above 15%, well above the level consistent with stability. The ratio of pay between the top and the bottom is currently well above 100:1, more than double the typical pattern of the 1950s and 1960s.

Alongside these new indicators, the government should identify the most effective policy instruments for reaching these targets. These need to be designed to restrict the level of economic inequality to within the limits that prevent instability. They would range from tax and industrial policy to the role of collective bargaining and corporate governance. When the targets are breached – as they clearly are at the moment – then policy needs to be adjusted accordingly.

The key lesson of the last 30 years is that economies that allow the richest members of society to accumulate a larger and larger share of the cake merely brings a dangerous mix of demand deflation, asset appreciation and a long squeeze on the productive economy that will end in economic turmoil. Social democracy's traditional belief in more equal societies is not just a matter of fairness and social justice, it is also a necessary condition for economic success.

NOTES

1. L. von Mises, *Ideas on Liberty,* New York: Irvington, 1955; chapter 9
2. K. Joseph, *Stranded on the Middle Ground,* London: Centre for Policy Studies, 1976

3. A. Okun, *Equality and Efficiency: The Big Tradeoff*, Washington DC: Brookings Institute Press, 1975

4. S. Lansley, *The Cost of Inequality: Why Greater Equality is Essential for Recovery*, London: Gibson Square, 2012; chapter 6

5. A.G. Berg and J.D. Ostry, 'Equality and Efficiency', *Finance and Development*, IMF, September 2011

6. See, for example, the *Hutton Review of Fair Pay, Interim Report*, London: Treasury, 2010; pp.27–30

7. E. Saez, *Striking it Richer: The Evolution of Top Incomes in the United States* (Updated with 2009 and 2010 estimates), 2 March 2012, available at: http://elsa.berkeley.edu/~saez/saez-UStopincomes-2010.pdf

8. A. Smith, *The Wealth of Nations*, Book III, Chapter IV, Oxford: Clarendon Press, 1976; p.448

Chapter 3

FROM UK PLC TO CO-OP UK

Transforming the Private Sector

Bill Kerry

A word-search of the 2010 Labour manifesto does not make happy reading for those of us who wish to see greater economic democracy wedded to social democracy.[1] The word 'co-operative' is rarely mentioned and even then it is only in connection with small-scale economic or social activity or transforming schools. The term 'employee-owned' is mentioned once, although the manifesto did want to see a step-change in their role in the economy. The terms 'mutual' and 'social enterprise' were also mentioned a handful of times but this was mostly related to transforming public services. Overall, the role envisaged for such stakeholder businesses was extremely limited and focused far more towards reforming the public sector rather than galvanizing the private sector. This timid thinking still lives on in the Blair-ish wing of the Labour Party, as witnessed by *The Purple Book* in 2011. Tristram Hunt's chapter eloquently boosts the cause of economic democracy, but overall the book still betrays a lack of ambition as to the scale of change needed, as well as a lack of direction such that attention is too focused on perceived problems in the public sector and not enough on actual (and more serious) failings in the private sector.[2]

This timidity is all very strange when we consider that the Co-operative Party is an historic and affiliated part of the Labour Party. Many Labour MPs, including the current shadow chancellor, sit in its name. There is clearly no great political will in the Labour Party to put co-operation at the heart of an alternative, progressive economic policy. This is a great shame. If it did summon up the courage it would have a ready-made 'big idea' that could inform set-piece political speeches, provide an overarching narrative and provide the basis for the launch of the next general election manifesto and probably several after that.

THE ANSWER UNDER OUR NOSES

It would be hugely encouraging to hear Ed Miliband talking about building a 'people's economy', echoing the highly successful Swedish Social Democratic concept of a 'people's home'. He could set an ambitious stretch-target for a certain percentage of the value of the private sector being owned by either customers and/or employees by, say, 2025. This way he would be putting co-operative, mutual and employee-owned businesses front and centre in Labour's economic strategy, rather than keeping them hidden away on the fringes as they are now.

This isn't mere ideology or utopianism, it is common sense. Co-operation works, even in the toughest circumstances. One of the few economic success stories of recent times has been the growth and resilience of businesses that are either owned by their employees or their customers (or both) rather than by shareholders and which have social goals in mind as well as profit-maximizing.

The annual report of Co-ops UK for 2012 notes that there are '... now more than 5,900 co-operative businesses in the UK [that] contribute £35.6bn to the UK economy and operate across all business sectors. For the past four years, the sector has outperformed the UK economy, demonstrating resilience in difficult economic times and proving that values and principles go hand in hand with commercial performance.'[3]

And it's not just co-ops bucking the generally gloomy economic trends. Social Enterprise UK reported in its *Fightback Britain* report in 2011 that the social enterprise sector was still growing and was outperforming the small- and medium-sized private business sector.[4] Meanwhile, Mutuo, an organization which seeks specifically to promote mutual economic and social activity, notes that since 2001 '... more than a million citizens have become members of new mutuals' (although it should be noted that some of this boost will have come from mutualizing services that were previously under public ownership).[5]

Then there are employee-owned businesses. Research by Cass Business School in 2010 found that employee-owned firms created new jobs more quickly than conventionally structured businesses (they recruit more employees at a faster rate and reward employees with higher wages) and are as profitable as conventional businesses. In addition, their performance is more stable over business cycles and they have outperformed the market during the downturn. They were also found to be more robust and have a lower risk of business failure.[6]

The relative economic success of these stakeholder models amidst the current economic malaise provides compelling evidence that the public favours them as providers of goods and services. This is supported by research carried out by Co-ops UK in 2010 which found that co-operatives were viewed favourably as being local, based on sharing profits, honest, trusted and a good way to run a business. PLCs meanwhile were widely associated with being global (74%), being cut throat (56%) and being greedy (55%).[7]

Put simply, stakeholder businesses are economically successful and the general public likes them. It is hard to see how these factors, taken together, would not automatically deliver the keys to No. 10 Downing Street to any party leader bold enough to seize the initiative and put them at the heart of their economic strategy. And they would need to be very bold indeed – bolder in fact than Margaret Thatcher was in the 1980s. The scale of change I am suggesting would be of that sort of order but almost certainly without the major backers in industry, finance and the media who boosted her project.

Powerful vested interests would have to be taken on and faced down at home and great thought would need to be given to the challenge of sustaining investment in such a radically different economic model. Meanwhile, abroad, there may well be issues with EU competition law if any UK government was seen to be favouring a certain sector of the economy over another. A move away from UK plc towards Co-operative UK would very likely fare better if it had the support of our progressive European partners, particularly those in France and Germany.

BUT WHAT ABOUT THE STATE?

Perhaps I have now set some sort of record by getting this far into an article about social democracy without mentioning the state – which is rather my point. Of course, we must continue to advance the arguments for the state's active role in the economy and our society. We can engage in the debate about stakeholder models being used in the public sector but we should be clear that such innovations must be about service improvement through employee empowerment, proper participation in decision making and job enrichment. It must not be merely a stepping stone to eventual privatization. Cast iron asset locks will be required guaranteeing reversion to public owner-ship in the event of service failure. And if we take part in this debate why not renew the case for public ownership more generally, and especially in those sectors of the economy where privatization has clearly failed (railways) or where long-term strategic interests are not being properly managed (energy).

But we must not allow ourselves to become completely consumed by debates about the extent and nature of the state's role in our economy and society. We have to think a lot more about the private sector and, in particular, its ownership. I would argue that we need to set about transforming the private sector such that it becomes far more sympathetic and supportive of social democratic ideals and goals. We need to think about the state *and* the private sector. Currently social democracy resembles only half a theory and we des-perately need a whole one.

The stakeholder business sector, outlined above, means we already have a substantial edifice on which social democrats could seek to base a transformation in the private sector. These businesses are largely successful, stable and are more in tune with social democratic values of fairness and equality. Their more democratic and participa-tive structures tend to restrain executive pay at the top and generally compress pay ratios between the highest and lowest paid (although the recent dispute between the retailer John Lewis and its outsourced cleaners is a stark reminder that stakeholder businesses are not always perfect and that strong trade unions will always be needed).

If we choose not to engage with the private sector and do not seek to fundamentally change its composition then I fear we may be fighting an eternal losing battle in trying to defend public services and the welfare state. We need to face up to the fact that there is an increasing tendency for the private sector to seek refuge in lucrative public contracts at national, regional and local level. This is a real game-changer for social democrats.

Aided and abetted by politicians across all the mainstream parties and urged on by various centrist and right-wing think tanks as well as cheerleaders in the media, an increasing number of large private sector companies now clearly see the state as one vast opportunity to make fairly easy and secure money over very long periods. Why do the hard and expensive version of capitalism involved in, say, manufacturing when you can do an easier and cheaper version administering assets and services already built up and paid for over decades by taxpayers?

MEET THE PUBLIC SERVICES INDUSTRY (PSI)

The state has always contracted with the private sector but this practice has grown enormously in recent decades. In a 2008 report by Dr DeAnne Julius, for the then Labour government, it was noted that PSI in the UK was the second largest in the world after its equivalent in the USA. It accounted for nearly 6% of GDP having grown 130% over the previous 12 years albeit with slowed growth towards the end of that period. Its revenues totalled £79 billion in 2007–8 and the largest sectors within PSI were health (£24.2bn) followed by social protection (£17.9bn), defence (£10.1bn) and education (£7.3bn).[8]

As we are paying for all this we should probably be taking a close interest in how our money is being used and, in particular, how it is being distributed. PSI does generate employment, an impressive 1.2 million staff at the time of the Julius report, but it is clear that the vast majority of people employed by PSI do very difficult jobs for very low wages. This does not, however, seem to apply to PSI senior management.

In a 2011 report by the campaign group One Society, entitled *A Third of A Percent* (highlighting the fact that FTSE 100 companies, on average, valued their lowest paid staff at 0.3% of the value attributed to their Chief Executives), the PSI data were particularly striking. It is clear that what they pay their CEOs is far in excess of any comparable role in the public sector. The report estimated that none of the PSI companies surveyed paid their CEOs less than 59 times UK median earnings whereas the public sector is now expected, after the Hutton Fair Pay Review, to be moving towards pay ratios – top to bottom – of no more than 1:20.[9] PSI therefore appears to be an aggravating factor when it comes to the UK's high level of income inequality and our growing problem with low pay that is locking so many of our fellow citizens out of the chance of a decent life.

A word of caution here, PSI should probably not be seen in isolation from the trends begun in the 1980s towards the privatization of state assets and services and which were then developed through such mechanisms as private–public partnerships and private-finance initiatives.[10] Taken altogether these developments are perhaps best seen as a broad response of a capitalist system that has been under pressure for several decades and is now seeking ways to maintain revenues and profitability in the face of increasingly competitive and difficult global economic circumstances. This impulse is surely only going to become more aggressive the longer the world economy continues to flatline. It's cold out there and burrowing into the warm fabric of the state is clearly a very attractive option for many companies and individuals with any surplus capital to invest.

The evidence to date suggests that the UK political mainstream is more than happy to accommodate private companies seeking this sort of corporate welfare. PSI expanded massively under New Labour governments and this has continued apace under the Coalition's Big Society initiative and its Open Public Services agenda, which makes it clear that almost any public service can be provided by any qualified provider. A key contributor to these developments has been the inability of social democracy, both as a current within the Labour and Liberal Democrat parties and as a broader intellectual tradition, to offer a viable and attractive alternative vision of society.

FROM REFORM TO TRANSFORMATION

Good politics cannot be just about managing the present, it has to be about painting a picture of a better society – a better world – and then showing people how we might get there. That's what makes people join political parties, get out there on the doorsteps and get the votes in. To rejuvenate social democracy we need to spend much more time setting out our own vision of how people's lives can be made better and far less time responding to a failing centre-right economic and social agenda. We need to actively promote alternatives in every area of debate, from general principles through to detailed policies. They say compete, we say co-operate; they say reform public services, we say improve public services; and when they say low taxes, we say fair taxes.

Beyond this, social democrats must move to fuse the red and green agendas into a coherent and easily understandable narrative. Across the developed world, we need to work hard to shift thinking from the increasingly useless economic growth paradigm towards a new one of improved well-being founded on greater equality of outcomes.[11] We know that we don't need a bigger pie, we just need to share it out far more equitably – within the developed world and globally from north to south. That way we can live well and all within planetary limits. We will not need to cross our fingers and simply hope that the owners of capital eventually pluck up courage to invest in very expensive (and uncertain) technological fixes for our mounting environmental problems.

The idea I have tried to outline above is that social democracy needs economic democracy in order to make it a coherent and complete theory of society. This means we must have a deliberate project to create a transformed private sector that can work in harmony with a robust, enabling and caring state. If we do not have such a plan for the private sector, I fear we will be eternally on the back foot. We will waste all our energies refuting the erroneous and tedious 'private sector good, public sector bad' narrative which is relentlessly boosted by the political Right in the interests of their wealthy friends. We will have to continue forever circling the wagons and justifying the role of the state while predatory private interests relentlessly pick away at our public assets and services. This will lock social democracy permanently into where it is now, a backward-looking and defensive-sounding politics – long on proud history but short on inspiring vision.

Without a grand vision and a sense of direction social democracy will remain a static and essentially reformist political doctrine, primarily concerned with how the state can ameliorate and contain the excesses of the market. It will be fighting twenty-first century battles with nineteenth- and twentieth-century weapons. All will be lost. If, on the other hand, social democracy becomes a transformative political creed that seeks, very clearly, to take us on a journey towards the Good Society based squarely on economic and social equality and environmental sustainability, then it has every chance of prospering.

NOTES

1. The Labour Party Manifesto 2010 – *A Future Fair for All*, www.labour.org.uk/labours-manifesto-for-a-future-fair-for-all

2. R. Philpot (ed.), *The Purple Book: A Progressive Future for Labour*, London: Biteback, 2011

3. From the website of Co-ops UK introducing its annual report, *The UK Co-operative Economy 2012*, www.uk.coop/economy2012

4. From *Fightback Britain: A Report on the State of Social Enterprise Survey 2011*, published by Social Enterprise UK and available at: www.socialenterprise.org.uk/advice-support/resources

5. From the website of Mutuo – www.mutuo.co.uk/about

6. From the report *Model Growth: Do Employee-owned Businesses Deliver Sustainable Performance?* (2010) carried out by the Cass Business School and available on the website of the Employee Ownership Association at: www.employeeownership.co.uk/publications

7. From the report *Good Business? Public Perceptions of Co-operatives* (2010) by Giles Simon and Ed Mayo, available on the Co-ops UK website at: www.uk.coop/resources/documents

8. From the *Public Services Industry Review (2008)* by Dr DeAnne Julius, available on the website of the Department for Business, Innovation and Skills at: www.bis.gov.uk/analysis/economics/public-services-industry-review

9. From the One Society report *A Third of a Percent: The Pay of UK Low-paid Workers Compared to that of Their CEOs (2011)*, available at: www.onesociety.org.uk/research/pay-ratios

10. Professor Dexter Whitfield's book *Global Auction of Public Assets, Nottingham: Spokesman, 2010* is trenchant on this point

11. R. Wilkinson and K. Pickett, *The Spirit Level*, London: Penguin, 2010

Chapter 4

THE ENVIRONMENT

From Unrestrained Markets to a Green Economy

Michael Meacher MP

The evidence that current trends in both the global economy and environment are unsustainable can hardly be doubted. The combined pincer impact on the Earth's carrying capacity of oil and water shortages, population overreach, global warming and climate turmoil, and the limit on resource availability in relation to the demands made upon it are broadly understood, yet far too little averting action is taken despite ever-sharper warnings from the scientists. How can this impasse be broken?

THE ORIGINS OF THE ENVIRONMENTAL CRISIS

The magnitude of the global economic crisis is all too painfully recognized, but the environmental crisis is much greater. A European study of ecosystems in 2008–9 estimated the losses from the financial crash at $2–3 trillion while the loss of natural capital *from deforestation alone* was calculated at $2–5 trillion *every year.*[1] This total was reached by estimating the value of the services, such as locking up carbon and providing fresh water, which forests provide, and then calculating the costs of either replacing them or living without them.

Though both crises are seen very differently, they actually derive from the same basic cause. Those who have engaged in the exploitation, whether of financial artefacts or natural resources, have demanded unsustainable rates of return and invoked indebtedness that is unrepayable, whilst living in denial of the inevitable consequences of impending dislocation. At first the resources appear inexhaustible. Then the long-term trend of depletion is fudged over by fluctuations which provide short-term confidence that disaster can be averted. Meanwhile, a powerful elite consolidate their interests which, though built on precarious foundations, they defend ferociously. Then as reality gradually exposes that previous assurances were false, promises are given that technology and innovation will solve all problems. Cutting down the last tree on Easter Island has its parallel in draining the last, deepest oil-well five miles below the sea, the more so when the global population to be serviced will soon be a million times greater than the Pacific atoll.

We are now at the stage of easy promises that give false assurance. We are told that we can paint growth green, the beguiling idea that under the rubric of 'sustainable development' the economy, society and environment can be given equal weight, whereas in practice of course economic growth always trumps the other two variables. We are assured that we can continue the maximum feasible extraction and utilization of fossil fuel energy because geoengineering can either blot out or counteract any increase in global warming or carbon emissions, when such attempts to transform the atmosphere or climate are puny relative to the scale of the growing greenhouse gas emissions to be contained (over 35bn tonnes this year). We are told that clever technology can decouple growth from environmental impacts; in fact average global carbon intensity would have to be 130 times lower by mid-century to meet climate goals, falling from 770 grams of CO_2 per dollar of output today to just 6 grams by 2050 – a scenario that is risible.

The business-as-usual programme is therefore bankrupt. But having said that, the forces of resistance and denial remain extraordinarily strong. The alliance of the US political class with the oil industry, the view of almost all the developing countries that ending poverty is more important than fighting climate change, and the lack of inspired and determined political leadership almost everywhere have all played a role. But the fundamental underlying constraint has been the iron grip, until now, of the neo-liberal financial agenda with its unremitting emphasis on unfettered markets, endless growth, competitiveness, deregulation, and the consolidation of Western global power around the Washington Consensus.

THE TIDE BEGINS TO TURN

But many of these factors are now changing. China and India are already, even if not signatories to the Kyoto Protocol, taking extensive action to curb emissions partly out of fear that they themselves could be major victims of the ravages of climate change and partly because of public revolt against hugely polluted cities. Political leadership is still feeble, but the increasing frequency and ferocity of extreme weather conditions, especially if more Katrina-type hurricanes savage the wealthy rather than the poor world, is slowly pushing this issue higher up the political agenda.

But by far the most important change lies in the collapse of the neo-liberal financialized world order in the decade-long depression after 2007. It has opened the eyes of the public to the downsides and inequities of unlimited wealth creation and has exposed hidden detriments that have long existed but were previously ignored or dismissed. They include the ill-effects of ballooning inequality at both domestic and international levels, the dangerous tensions over shrinking energy and other scarce resources that could lead to war, and the risks of pushing the international economy over the edge where climate catastrophe becomes irreversible.

There are other developments too, prompted by the 2008–9 economic collapse, which are relevant here. It has brought to the fore the fundamental issue: what is growth for? The New Economics Foundation in particular has drawn attention to the range of international surveys indicating that beyond an annual income of some $15,000 per head, life satisfaction scarcely changes between countries with very different GDP levels. In other words, there seems to be a definite level beyond which extra income doesn't deliver extra well-being. This is less surprising than it might seem. GDP is a concept promoted by economic elites because its distributional effects are strongly skewed to serve their own interests. But it is an unsuitable measure on several grounds. It does not distinguish between income and capital, thus enabling the liquidation of natural resources and mounds of unsustainable credit to be treated as growth. It masks vast gulfs of inequality as per capita statistics. And it takes the market valuation of prices as a datum, though both the financial crash and the decoupling of wealth from happiness should make us deeply wary of any such assumption.

If human well-being rather than GDP is the ultimate objective, the relevant measure is the efficiency with which fundamental inputs into the economy, such as natural resources from an over-stretched biosphere, are transformed into desirable and meaningful human outcomes in the form of relatively long and satisfied lives. By that criterion some striking conclusions emerge. Contrary to the conventional eulogy for successful, knowledge-driven, resource-light service economies, the core European countries have in general become less carbon-efficient in securing well-being for their citizens than in the 1960s. Equally significantly, while people in the UK and Europe report comparable standards of well-being whether they have high-consuming and resource-intensive lifestyles or low-consuming with a much smaller ecological footprint, the former would require 6½ planets if pursued worldwide while the latter might fit into the one planet we actually have.

The implications of this analysis are huge. It implies that lower consumption need not undermine quality of life and that govern-ments' fear of demand management may be greatly exaggerated. It explains why the Anglo-Saxon economic model is shown as the least efficient among 30 countries analysed, with Scandinavia revealed as the most efficient in delivering the highest levels of well-being in Europe at low environmental cost. So the problem isn't just the relentless running down of natural capital (already at some 130% of the reproduction rate of the planet), nor the scarcity of key resources such as water or oil, nor even the overshadowing threat of climate turmoil. It's rather that the dynamics of the international economy are generating diminishing returns for what should be the central objective of the economy – maximizing quality of life, well-being and happiness spread as equally as possible across the world.

The global media now disseminate the ubiquitous subliminal message that to be seen, heard, respected and loved, you need the right trainers, jeans, toys and gadgets. But such consumption only breeds yet more competitiveness and envy which makes children and young people feel more isolated, insecure and unfulfilled, thus unleashing yet more frantic consumption in an endless vicious cycle. Confronting the costs of capitalist growth certainly means chal-lenging and dismantling the insidious culture of consumerism. As Wilkinson and Pickett have so poignantly shown in *The Spirit Level*, it means recognizing that stark income inequality rather than the lack of higher GDP are what lies behind so much social pathology – loss of trust, mental ill-health, higher rates of murder and violence, lower life expectancy, drug use, poor educational attainment, obesity, and so much else.[2] If, then, endless growth is to be dethroned as the overriding objective of industrialized economies, a new ecological macroeconomics is needed to scale investments in terms of resource efficiency, clean technologies and ecosystem enhancement.

THE SHIFT TO A SUSTAINABLE WORLD

So how can such a vast transformation come about? One answer is that, whatever humans may or may not decide it will be implemented by natural forces, even brutally or violently, because the indefinite persistence of current trends is ruled out. In a world of 9–10 billion people by 2050, all aspiring to a level of income equal to an average EU income with 2% annual growth built in, carbon intensities would have to be reduced by an average 11% a year to *stabilize* the climate, which is 16 times faster than has actually happened since the 1990 Kyoto Protocol base year. The truth is there is no credible, socially just, ecologically sustainable scenario of continually growing incomes on a planet carrying 9–10 billion people, and the facile assumption that capitalism's knack for innovation and ingenuity can somehow pull off the trick is sheer fantasy, given the colossal and ever-growing scale of the outcome required.

Perhaps recognizing this, industrial–financial leaders, looking to every device which can maintain their dominance based on its previous foundations, have come up with the answer of 'decoupling', meaning that economic growth can continue unabated so long as there is continually declining material throughput. Yet even *relative* decoupling has been falling worldwide since 2000 in some key structural materials such as iron ore, bauxite and cement. But what is far more of concern is that *absolute* decoupling – that is, overall reduction in resource throughput – has virtually not happened at all. Such improvements in energy and carbon intensity as have been achieved over the last two decades have been swamped by the increase in the scale of economic activity over the same period. Thus global carbon emissions from energy use have actually *risen* over this period by 40%.

Another related answer put forward to this underlying conundrum is a low-carbon economy. Yet again the sheer magnitude appears far out of reach. The seminal report Climate Solutions 2 estimated that some 20 clean energy, energy efficiency, low-carbon agriculture and sustainable forestry sectors will need to grow by 20–24% every year for the next four decades if greenhouse gas emissions are to be stabilized, yet only three of these sectors are on track.

The much more radical solution of a steady-state economy has been proposed by the environmental economist Herman Daly.[3] By this he means an economy with constant population and constant stock of capital, maintained by a low rate of throughput which the ecosystem can assimilate and regenerate. Low production rates would then equal low depreciation rates. Several mechanisms would implement this, including a cap-auction-trade system for basic resources, which would limit the scale of resource extraction whilst at the same time allowing efficient allocation through trading. Supplementary to that, ecological tax reform would shift the tax base from value added (labour and capital) and on to resources extracted from nature, put through the economy, and returned back to nature (pollution). The remaining commons of natural capital such as rainforests and the atmosphere would be protected by public trusts.

Further reforms would include dividing GDP in the national accounts between a cost account and a benefits account. The implicit logic of this would be a signal to stop growing when marginal costs equal marginal benefits. At the macro level, international commerce would be re-regulated to make the shift away from untrammelled free trade, free capital mobility and globalized exploitation. The present IMF–World Bank–WTO framework would be shifted towards Keynes' plan for a multilateral payments-clearing union, charging penalty rates on surplus as well as on deficit balances. The banking system would be moved towards 100% reserve requirements in place of the present fractional reserve banking, and control of the money supply would be taken back from the private banks and restored to government.

Radical as this transitional programme may appear, it is still based on the conservative institutions of private property and decentralized market allocation. But it does recognize that private property loses its legitimacy if it is too unequally distributed, and that markets lose their legitimacy too if they fail to reveal the full truth about costs. By the same token the macroeconomy also becomes untenable if its scale demands growth that exceeds the biophysical capacities of the Earth.

THE POLITICS OF TRANSITION

It must be admitted, however, that given the iron grip of the neo-liberal ideology on the public imagination, social culture and political consciousness, it is highly unlikely that such a transformation on the necessary scale would be attempted until a catastrophe, or more likely a series of catastrophes (as with the Pharaonic plagues in ancient Egypt), made clear beyond any doubt that continuing with business-as-usual was impossible and that minor adjustments to existing practices – already under way – would not cope either. At that point, likely within the next century, the choice will be either to continue as before and undergo continent-wide dislocation and an enormous decline in the global population (which the highly respected scientist James Lovelock puts at 90%) or to flip to a wholly different paradigm of interconnecting ecological strictures. It has happened several times in Earth's history, and human beings are quite capable of the hubris to bring it about once more.

To forestall this environmental Armageddon, several studies have sought to navigate a comprehensive transition consistent with commercial principles and involving minimum disruption. Nicholas Stern's *A Blueprint for a Safer Planet* sets out systematically, as the former chief economist to the UK Treasury, the case that high-carbon growth will eventually self-destruct as fossil fuel prices rise sharply and the physical destructiveness of climate change begins to bite widely and deeply.[4] Lester Brown's Plan B in *World on the Edge* proposes, as a UN economist, a new infrastructure based on true-cost accounting with honest markets and a fivefold increase in the use of renewable energy, plus detailed research on restoring natural support systems, eradicating poverty, stabilizing populations, rescuing failed state, and feeding 8–9 billion people.[5] Tim Jackson's *Prosperity without Growth* questions whether growth is still a legitimate goal for rich countries now at all, not just because of the ecological constraints but for reasons of human happiness, and seeks to weaken the link between rising incomes and human well-being as much as on the imperatives of environmental limits.[6]

It is a sad fact that has to be faced that these brave efforts to draw up a reasoned path to fundamental change, a relatively smooth transition rather than the cliff edge that will sooner or later be faced by unyielding intransigence, have been successively blocked by political barriers. The all-encompassing intense US–China rivalry was the central factor that stalled the post-Rio 'green' momentum, most notably at the 2009 Copenhagen international negotiations. Linked with that, the huge political muscle and lobbying power of the fossil fuel and nuclear industries, in contrast to a weak and fragmented renewable industry, has repeatedly cowed governments into submission to their demands, most strikingly with the (false) claim that without their total co-operation 'the lights will go out'. This power structure has then relentlessly fed the canard that an environmental transition would be risky, expensive, unnecessary, and threaten today's comforts and pleasures. This combined array of forces has prevented the build-up of the critical mass of public support needed to override the usual caution of the political class.

What is ironic, if not tragic, about this stasis is that the UK is better placed, because of its island location in the eastern Atlantic, to exploit wind power and wave and tidal power than any other EU country, yet is gratuitously passing up both the economic and environmental benefits this would bring. It generates only 5% of its electricity from renewables, less than any other EU country except Malta and Luxemburg, and well short of the 10–25% achieved by Germany, France, Italy and Spain, and far short of Scandinavia's 35–50%. Contrary to natural geographical potential, Germany had by 2008 created 249,000 jobs in the renewable energy sector with a turnover of €24 billion, compared with Britain's just 7,000 jobs and a turnover of only €0.3 billion. Spain has made thermal energy resources compulsory in new and refurbished buildings, whilst in the UK the feed-in tariff rates were abruptly halved in 2012, which flattened an emerging solar power industry, lost 5,000 jobs, and led to the import of Chinese solar panels instead.

Equally, the UK has the best marine energy resource in Europe, with the potential to supply 20% of current electricity demand and create 10,000 jobs by 2020, yet the £50 million marine renewable deployment fund was closed down in 2011. UK governments have declared themselves keen to promote carbon capture and storage (CCS) technology, yet have continued to dither and have allowed Canada and Australia and 20 other demonstration projects worldwide to get ahead first. The correct decision to abandon the third runway at Heathrow is clearly now being U-turned which will hugely increase carbon emissions, pollution and congestion without any prospect of long-term sustainability. And the Green Deal, trumpeted to create 100,000 insulation jobs by 2015 and reach 24 million homes by 2020, has now been cut back to one-fifth or less of that number, while fuel poverty is expected to nearly double by 2016.

The prospects for environmental renewal are enormous if only Britain, still in thrall to an unsustainable 'ancien regime', can break free. Making that break will be one of Labour's biggest challenges.

NOTES

1. P. Sukhdev, *The Economics of Ecosystems and Biodiversity*, Deutsche Bank, European Report, 2008
2. R. Wilkinson and K. Pickett, *The Spirit Level: Why Equality is Better for Everyone*, London: Allen Lane, 2010
3. H. Daly, *A Steady State Economy*, London: Sustainable Development Commission, 2009
4. N. Stern, *A Blueprint for a Safer Planet: How to Manage Climate Change and Create a New Era of Progress and Prosperity*, London: Bodley Head, 2009
5. L. Brown, *World on the Edge: How to Prevent Environmental and Economic Collapse*, London: Earthscan, 2011
6. T. Jackson, *Prosperity without Growth? The Transition to a Sustainable Economy*, London: Sustainable Development Commission, 2009

Chapter 5

SOCIAL DEMOCRACY, INDUSTRIAL DEMOCRACY AND RESPONSIBLE CAPITALISM

David Coats

INTRODUCTION

For more than 30 years the case for industrial democracy has been kept firmly off the political agenda. The last effort by the 1974–9 Labour government, the Bullock report (1977), was met with profound employer hostility and union opposition or indifference. Businesses were apparently concerned that workers' representatives on boards would impose unacceptable constraints on the ability of managers to take tough decisions. Trade unions, on the other hand, were worried that their independence might be compromised by accepting a seat at the directors' table – many, and not just those on the Left, had no wish to be complicit in management decisions.

After the Winter of Discontent and the defeat of the Callaghan government public policy sought to turn back the clock rather than consolidate the gains of the postwar era. The Thatcher and Major governments saw trade union power as the principal source of Britain's economic problem rather than as part of the solution. Vigorously expressed hostility to organized labour was an article of faith for most Conservatives during this period.

Post-1997 New Labour made the legislative environment slightly less hostile for trade unions – introducing a new trade union recognition procedure and belatedly implementing the EU directive on information and consultation – but was unwilling to countenance a wider discussion about power in the workplace or more generally in the labour market. This was despite the efforts of the TUC under the leadership of John Monks to promote a defiantly European model of social partnership. From 1994 to 2003 British trade unions were committed, at least in principle, to the notion that a robust bargaining relationship with employers could be complemented by a more collaborative approach to solving shared problems. Moreover, this model of workplace partnership was part of a wider agenda to develop effective institutions for social dialogue with both government and employers at national and European level.

Central to the TUC's approach was the belief that poor economic and social outcomes were a consequence of the short-term thinking endemic in British capitalism. For many senior executives their overarching goal was (and remains) the maximization of shareholder value. This led inevitably to the conceptualization of the corporation as a portfolio of assets to be traded or managed. Chief executives built their reputations on the execution of mergers and acquisitions. The idea that a company might succeed through building its capabilities over the long term and by offering high-quality goods and services to consumers appeared odd, alien or utopian to many of the inhabitants of Britain's boardrooms. That was why Tony Blair's notorious call for a 'stakeholder' economy, delivered in Singapore in 1995, seemed to be a radical departure from previous thinking – although the idea was quickly dropped when the extent of business hostility became clear.

Now, the situation is very different. The market fundamentalist model that appeared so robust in the late 1990s is exceedingly threadbare today. Some of the consequences of the Thatcher–Major policy reforms, most notably the apparently inexorable rise in income inequality, are seen as sources of economic instability rather than as wellsprings of prosperity. Public revulsion at corporate excess has encouraged the Coalition government to consider measures to restrain the increases in executive pay, improve the transparency of corporate reporting and limit the scope for short-termism in British equity markets.

What the Coalition has not done, however, is recognize that power and influence in the workplace and the wider labour market affect management behaviour, the distribution of incomes, the motivation of the workforce and the performance of business. This leaves Labour with an opportunity to return to arguments of principle about the relationship between social democracy and industrial democracy and to develop a coherent, distinctive model of responsible capitalism, one which explains how British businesses can succeed at the same time as desirable social outcomes are achieved.

WHAT DO WE MEAN BY INDUSTRIAL DEMOCRACY?

Before we turn to the development of the policy agenda it is important to define the notion of industrial democracy and explain why it matters to social democrats. In the 1970s the answer was clear: industrial democracy meant workers on the board and the goal was the modernization of British industrial relations. Yet industrial democracy could be said to embrace a much wider range of possibilities including: strong collective bargaining and workplace representation models; mutual and co-operative forms of ownership; an explicit, radical notion of workers' control; statutory information and consultation with workers' representatives through works councils on the continental European model; various forms of employee share ownership; and, by stretching the argument a little, those models of supposedly enlightened human resource management that place a premium on individual employee involvement and employee engagement.

ARGUMENTS OF PRINCIPLE VERSUS PRAGMATIC/ INSTRUMENTAL ARGUMENTS

Most social democrats would agree that workers should not surrender their rights as citizens when they cross their employer's threshold. This means that workers continue to have the right to speak freely and to associate with people of like mind. International treaties and conventions confirm the point. The UN's Universal Declaration of Human Rights embraces free speech, freedom of association and the right to establish collective bargaining. The European Convention on Human Rights is drafted in similar terms, as is the EU's Declaration of Fundamental Rights. The so-called 'core' conventions of the International Labour Organization prohibit child labour and forced labour at the same time as they guarantee the rights to organize and bargain collectively.

It is clear that these rights have already been recognized by policy makers as important, but why are they fundamental? There are two potential answers. The first has liberal roots but should be valued by social democrats nonetheless, whereas the second is founded on a more straightforward understanding of power relationships in the workplace.

First, it is wrong to treat workers simply as instruments that enable a corporation to achieve its ends. Workers are people, not 'human resources' or a peculiarly intractable factor of production. If citizens expect political decisions affecting them to be subject to the tests of justification (they have been explained) and legitimacy (they have been made following due process), why should different principles apply at work? Employers need more than employees' grudging acquiescence; high performance depends on workers' commitment and enthusiasm and this is most likely to be secured where decisions have been made following proper consultation, even if those affected are unhappy with the outcome.

Opponents of this argument will undoubtedly argue that companies are not democracies. It is not too fanciful to say that some chief executives find more inspiration in the pre-revolutionary France of Louis XIV than in the rights-based thinking of the Enlightenment. According to this view the imperious CEO should be empowered to act as if 'l'entreprise c'est moi', workers should do as they are told and be grateful for the privilege of a job. This may sound surprising, but there are plenty of British business people who express similar thoughts, albeit in the less extravagant language of 'leadership' or 'management's right to manage'.

The second answer is derived from the fundamental imbalance of power inscribed in the employment relationship. The employer is a collective but the worker is an individual. The employer can fire an employee and find a replacement without too much difficulty, whereas an employee who is dismissed must take their chances on the open labour market and experience a significant loss of income while they search for alternative employment. Otto Kahn-Freund, the eminent Anglo-German labour lawyer, put it like this:

[T]he relation between an employer and an isolated employee or worker is typically a relation between a bearer of power and one who is not a bearer of power. In its inception it is an act of submission, in its operation it is a condition of

subordination, however much the submission and subordination may be concealed by that indispensable figment of the
legal mind known as the 'contract of employment'.[1]

Industrial democracy is the instrument used to establish an appropriate balance of power in the workplace, whether through collective
bargaining or the statutory works councils mandated in many continental European countries. The important word here is balance;
employers and workers may sometimes find that their interests coin-
cide and sometimes find that they do not – conflict is therefore both
inevitable and legitimate. Indeed, one might argue that it is through
disagreement that each party begins to understand the other's point
of view, laying the foundations for a durable settlement. Of course, if
one side upsets the balance by becoming too powerful then the asymmetry of the relationship makes it much more difficult to achieve a
successful resolution.

It is worth recalling, perhaps, that social democracy's principal
purpose is to enlarge the sphere of freedom for citizens – to, using
slightly different language, ensure that people can acquire the capabilities they need to choose lives that they value. As others argue
elsewhere in this volume, greater equality is a prerequisite for more
extensive liberty. Social justice and freedom go hand-in-hand.
This implies too, of course, that people at work can never be more
than a means to achieve their employer's ends unless the fundamental inequalities of power in the workplace are recognized and
corrected.

THE BRITISH WORKPLACE TODAY: 'HARD TIMES' OR THE 'SUNLIT UPLANDS'?

We might worry a little less about the case for industrial democracy
if we could be confident that most British workplaces are open, par-
ticipative, not excessively hierarchical and are characterized by a
high level of trust. Unfortunately the evidence points in the opposite direction. Even the Chartered Institute of Personnel and
Development, which represents the 'human resource' profession,
admits that most employees have little faith in senior management.
A study commissioned by the Labour government found that around
one-third of employees had suffered some form of unfair treatment
in the previous two years – often beyond the limits of those matters

covered by employment rights. The national skills survey, sponsored by the Economic and Social Research Council, reported that most employees have less control over their working lives than was the case a decade ago, are working harder and rarely believe that their skills are being properly utilized. Industrial conflict has been displaced from the collective (negotiation between employers and trade unions, strikes and settlements) to the individual (the rising tide of individual applications to employment tribunals). Employers may complain about red tape and regulation but they have brought the situation upon themselves – if trade unions are not present to nip problems in the bud then workers have no alternative but to vindicate their statutory employment rights.

It is not entirely surprising therefore that the incidence of worker voice – the organized capacity to influence an employer's important decisions – is lower in the UK than in any other country of the EU 15. Perhaps trade unions did need reform at the end of the 1970s, but the relentless assault on organized labour pursued by the Thatcher and Major governments produced unintended consequences, which have proved to be just as disadvantageous to employers as they are to workers.

Nonetheless, there is strong evidence to show that people at work still understand the logic of collective action – the only way to change their employer's mind is to work with their colleagues. Thatcherism failed to generate a wave of individualism in the workplace that swept away the demand for worker voice. What can be said with some confidence, however, is that a collectivist orientation at work is not necessarily manifested as support for trade unionism. According to the TUC's own research, two-thirds of workers understand the fundamental truth of Kahn-Freund's observation, but barely one-third see a trade union as an effective vehicle for the expression of their views. More people at work today have never been members of a trade union than are either current members or ex-members. Organized labour's grip on most of the private sector has been weakening for some time. The challenge to union strategy, structure and culture is immense.

WORKER VOICE AND BUSINESS PERFORMANCE

Many employers resist the case for worker voice on the grounds that it is bad for business, bad for economic performance and therefore bad for workers. Once again, however, the evidence points in a rather different direction. Richard Freeman and James Medoff, in their classic study of the economic effects of unions in the USA, found that unions could be good for productivity, bad for productivity or have no impact at all.[2] The critical factor was the quality of the relationship that existed between a trade union, its members and the employer. More recent research in the UK has suggested that the highest trust workplace climate exists where there is a strong union, trusted by its members and respected by the employer.

German manufacturing industry remains the powerhouse of the eurozone despite the supposed burdens of workers' representatives on supervisory boards, the presence of works councils in the most successful companies and the widespread observance of collective agreements. The Nordic countries too, with their strong social democratic traditions, enjoyed levels of growth and employment during the boom years that either equalled or exceeded the performance of 'liberal' economies like the UK and the USA. And of course social outcomes in the Nordic countries remain the best in the world on the dimensions of poverty, income inequality and social mobility. There is no incompatibility between a powerful array of worker voice institutions and strong economic performance.

There has been much commentary over the last two years about the growth of the 'squeezed middle', the disconnection of wage growth from productivity growth and the obstacles that this places on the road to a robust economic recovery. While not quite endorsing all this story, both the IMF and the OECD have argued that rising income inequality was one of the causes of the crisis – because citizens accumulated excessive debts to maintain their lifestyles – and sustainable growth in the future depends on halting and reversing the trend. In other words, wages must rise in line with productivity to create the demand that keeps the economy on track. An IMF staff paper is quite explicit: the bargaining power of those on modest to low incomes must be improved.

A POLICY AGENDA FOR THE FUTURE

More then 35 years after Bullock, perhaps the time has come, therefore, to reopen the question of board composition and revisit the 'stakeholder' model outlined by Tony Blair in his Singapore speech. A great deal of ink has been spilt in analysing the short-termism of

British capital markets (and corporations), but taking specific action to ensure a wider range of voices are present in the boardroom could have a catalytic effect in generating more responsible behaviour. There must be an explicit recognition that the interests of the immediate body of shareholders may not be coextensive with the public interest or with the long-term interests of the company. Sovereign wealth funds and hedge funds, which now own a large slice of UK equities, may not be the best custodians of our economic future.

Precisely what form stakeholder representation might take and who needs to be represented remains an open question. Indeed, a durable settlement demands consensus and that in turn requires a public conversation rather than a partisan argument. Thoughtful Conservatives like Ferdinand Mount (a former director of Mrs Thatcher's No. 10 Policy Unit) have begun to see the wisdom of a two-tier board structure on the German model.[3] It would be odd for social democrats to be laggards in this developing debate.

A rebalancing of bargaining power may also have the incidental effect of imposing limits on top incomes. If workers are able to speak up collectively, the inhabitants of the UK's executive suites will find it difficult to apply one rule to their own pay and another to the pay of their employees. More effective worker voice is a more powerful instrument for restraining the exponential growth in executive pay than an annual shareholder vote on the report of the remuneration committee.

Given the weakness of trade unions in the private sector and the rising tide of 'never membership', Labour in government must think radically about how the state can facilitate the growth of powerful workplace institutions. Trade unions may not like it, but there is a persuasive case for learning from the works council models that are to be found in most of the other EU member states. Workers have enforceable legal rights to guarantee that they are participants in the decision-making process rather than simply victims of orders transmitted through the management chain. Indeed, trade unions may find some opportunities here – providing training, support and advice to members of works councils could prove to be a springboard for organization leading to the establishment of collective bargaining in a co-operative, high-trust framework of the kind that Freeman, Medoff and others have identified as essential for strong productivity and wage growth.

Much of this chapter has focused on the responsibilities of employers and unions. But social democrats should be committed to the notion that the state must be an exemplary employer and contractor too. From 1891–1983 this outcome was guaranteed by the various Fair Wages Resolutions of the House of Commons, which required all those supplying goods and services to the government to observe the relevant collective agreement (or the prevailing wage rates) in that business or industry. Reviving this approach today will require more creativity, not least because collective bargaining is conspicuous by its absence in most of the private sector. Perhaps the 'living wage' model, which requires all contractors (for either public or private sector clients) to pay a rate higher than the national minimum wage could be applied more systematically to public procurement. And where collective agreements do still exist they should be taken as the appropriate reference point.

By reviving the case for industrial democracy, social democrats are doing no more than being true to our values. The aspiration for an irreversible socialist transformation may have been abandoned but there is a great deal that can be done to achieve a more responsible capitalism, greater income equality and a richer notion of citizenship. By testing the market fundamentalist model to destruction our opponents have opened up political terrain that was abandoned for the last 30 years. The challenges are enormous – not least for the trade unions – but Labour's response to the crisis could set the UK on a different and more progressive course for at least a generation. Triangulation and moderately useful tinkering may have been the best we could have hoped for during the boom. Crisis conditions demand bolder action and the willingness to take political risks. Giving citizens real voice, power and influence in the workplace are essential for the UK to develop a sustainable model that secures growth, prosperity and opportunity for all.

NOTES

1. O. Kahn-Freund, *Labour and the Law*, 3rd edition (ed. P. Davies and M. Freedland), London: Stevens, 1983; p.18
2. R.B. Freeman and J.L. Medoff, *What Do Unions Do?* New York: Basic Books, 1984
3. F. Mount, *The New Few or A Very British Oligarchy: Power and Inequality in Britain Now*, London: Simon and Schuster, 2012

PART II

A SOCIAL DEMOCRATIC SOCIETY

Chapter 6

THE IMPORTANCE OF EQUALITY

Ruth Lister

Equality is at the heart of debates about what Labour stands for. An unequal society such as Britain in the early twenty-first century cannot be a genuinely social democratic society and it is certainly not a good society. Income inequality remains significantly higher than before it soared during the Thatcher years and is wide by international standards. Wealth is even more unevenly distributed. While there has been some reduction in cross-cutting inequalities associated with gender and ethnicity, they, together with others such as disability, remain deep-seated, shaping life chances and experiences.[1] This chapter begins with an overview of the main strands in Labour's debates about equality before making the case for why it is important. It concludes with some broad brush implications for policy and politics.

DEBATING EQUALITY

During the New Labour years the long-standing debate that pitted equality of opportunity against equality of outcome took centre stage. New Labour advocated equality of opportunity and Tony Blair in particular espoused a meritocratic model, which was developed under the auspices of the social mobility agenda (adopted too by the Conservative-led Coalition government). Under this model inequality as such is not considered to be a problem. What is at issue is who gets the attractive, well-rewarded positions, not the level at which those positions are rewarded or the overall hierarchy of rewards. Typically meritocrats deploy the metaphor of a ladder of opportunity and prioritize education and skills attainment as policy tools to enable those with merit to climb it. They ignore the ways in which the height of the ladder and the distance between its rungs affect how far people can climb. And they downplay the ways in which, at the bottom, poverty prevents some people even getting on to the ladder, while at the top privilege is deployed to protect against downwards mobility.

The meritocratic model suffers from a narrow market-oriented conception of merit. It does not question why, for instance, at the bottom of the ladder care work (largely done by women) is paid so little and at the top company executives or bankers (still mainly men) are paid so much. The ladder is not fashioned with reference to the contribution to society made by different kinds of work. It fails to acknowledge that not everyone wants to climb the ladder and that the ability to live a full and flourishing life should not be dependent on doing so.[2] Moreover, the meritocratic model tends to exacerbate inequality itself, both directly by fuelling a 'winner takes all' tendency and indirectly by legitimizing socioeconomic divisions. As Michael Young, who coined the term 'meritocracy', warned, the more that success is associated with merit and failure with lack of it, the easier it is to justify a huge economic gulf between those who succeed and those who don't. It also lends itself to New Labour's asymmetric emphasis on the responsibilities to society of those at the bottom while ignoring the responsibilities of those at the top.

Some of the limitations of the meritocratic model prompted New Labour theorists Anthony Giddens and Patrick Diamond to make the case for a 'new egalitarianism'. This shares with the meritocratic model a primary concern with the distribution of opportunities rather than of income and wealth. Nevertheless, it acknowledges that the one cannot be divorced from the other. Diamond and Giddens dismiss 'pure meritocracy' as 'incoherent because, without redistribution, one generation's successful individuals would become the next generation's embedded caste, hoarding the wealth they had accumulated'. And they accept that 'the promotion of equality of opportunity in fact requires greater material equality: it is impossible for individuals to achieve their full potential if social and economic starting-points are grossly unequal.'[3] This last point is given support by cross-national evidence, which indicates that generally levels of social mobility are greater and levels of poverty lower in more equal societies.

In contrast to the meritocratic and new egalitarian models, the case for greater equality as such is identified with what might be called 'real egalitarianism', the position adopted in this chapter. Real egalitarianism is concerned about the distribution of income and wealth. It shifts the focus from a concern with starting points to end results and from opportunities to rewards. Although it is sometimes parodied as advocating literal absolute equality of outcomes, in practice real egalitarians advocate greater equality than prevails at present, particularly in highly unequal societies like the UK. Real egalitarians are not arguing that everyone is or should be the same, as suggested by those who maintain equality stifles diversity. Some egalitarians therefore use terms such as 'equality of condition' to avoid the equation of equality with uniformity.

Others talk about equity as a better way of grasping the point that people are different and that the best way of achieving a more equal set of outcomes is not necessarily by treating everyone the same. This is particularly pertinent with reference to disabled people whose needs are greater than those of non-disabled people. Here the positions taken by egalitarian and meritocratic advocates can sometimes overlap, particularly through the latter's growing use of the capabilities approach developed by Amartya Sen and Martha Nussbaum.[4]

The capabilities approach focuses on the substantive freedom to live the kind of life one values and argues that income is no more than a means to this. Anthony Giddens has suggested that the approach offers a philosophical underpinning for meritocratic policies, particularly investment in education and skills.[5] More recently, a couple of contributors to *The Purple Book*, Patrick Diamond and Liam Byrne, have adopted the capabilities model in an attempt to move beyond the equality of opportunity versus outcome debate.[6] Diamond writes that it means treating people according to their different circumstances and does not require equality of outcome but instead empowers people to choose the outcomes of their own lives. Byrne translates capabilities into the language of power to argue that neither equality of opportunity nor equality of outcome is enough and that poverty is about more than low income. Instead the power or freedom to live the life one values is what counts. The emphasis on equality as positive freedom echoes the earlier arguments of egalitarians such as Roy Hattersley. However, while there is much of value in the capabilities approach, egalitarians need to guard against those who use it to downplay the importance of the underlying distribution of income and wealth, which either facilitates or constrains an individual's capabilities.

The most recent challenge to egalitarians from within the Labour Party comes from Blue Labour. Its leading exponent, Maurice Glasman, sums up its scepticism about the value of equality: 'Labour values are not abstract universal values such as "freedom" or "equality". Distinctive Labour values are rooted in relationships, in practices that strengthen an ethical life. Practices like reciprocity, which gives substantive form to freedom and equality in an active relationship of give and take.' Glasman decries Labour's espousal of such values, which apply in any society and are not specific to the political traditions of Britain. He calls on Labour to develop the idea of a good society 'built on relationships built on reciprocity, mutuality and solidarity'.[7] I find these arguments curious. It is not clear to me why 'equality' is a more abstract value than 'reciprocity', 'mutuality' and 'solidarity'. All such abstract values need to be translated into more concrete everyday language and illustrations, which speak to people's lives and hopes. And that is an important challenge for Labour. Reciprocity, mutuality and solidarity are all more likely to flourish in a more equal society, as I will argue further below. Equality thus represents an ethical stance with implications for how we live our lives, just as the values Glasman espouses do. Finally, while I share Blue Labour's scepticism about New Labour's starry-eyed obeisance to economic globalization, if one believes in internationalism then the values we espouse need to be universal, even if there is also room for the more parochial.

WHY EQUALITY MATTERS

Stewart Lansley makes the economic case for equality in Chapter 2. The importance of this case cannot be underestimated. Nevertheless, ultimately the economy is a means to an end and that end is a good society. Equality is a primary building block of a good society. As a material reality inequality is corrosive of such a society; it distorts our lives and our social and political relationships with each other. The ideal of equality offers us the hope of a better society and way of being. It also offers hope for the planet as it appears that more equal societies produce lower carbon footprints. A whole industry has grown up to help the rich spend their money, often in extremely ecologically irresponsible ways. Meanwhile, those in poverty, both domestically and globally, pay the highest price for climate change. Equality is thus central to notions of environmental justice.

Equality is also an essential element of the overarching value of social justice. Although some might dismiss social justice as simply another abstract concept, it has proved an effective mobilizing ideal both within nation states and globally. At its heart is a sense of fairness. While we do not all necessarily agree on what is fair, the social democratic case for equality is in part founded on the belief that it is unfair that any one group should enjoy disproportionate levels of income and wealth, which can buy opportunity, power and privilege. And it is unfair regardless of whether such rewards can be ascribed to luck (background or natural talent) or effort. Warren Buffet once observed that his enormous pay is 'no great credit' to himself: 'I was lucky at birth. I shouldn't delude myself into thinking I am some superior individual because of that.' Unfortunately, all too many of the high paid suffer from just such a delusion and use it to justify their enormous rewards. Moreover, even individual effort usually depends to some extent on the efforts of others. What politicians call 'rewards for success' may be easier to justify than 'rewards for failure', but the enormous differentials they create does not make this fair from an egalitarian perspective.

Research suggests that the general public is more likely to interpret fairness to be a matter of individual desert. Nevertheless, it also indicates that attitudes as to what constitutes desert can shift quite quickly – witness the reaction to the financial crisis as bankers were branded the undeserving rich. Moreover, individualistic notions of desert are not necessarily totally divorced from more relativistic and potentially egalitarian understandings. Research has revealed a perception that the contribution of the average worker is undervalued in comparison to that of the highly paid and that the distribution of rewards associated with different kinds of work does not always reflect what people consider to be fair. There is also evidence of considerable disquiet and indeed anger about excessively high levels of pay and the pay gap, rooted in beliefs about need as well as desert.[8] And most people would today accept that it is unfair if a person's gender, ethnicity, (dis)ability, age or sexuality (dis)advantaged them.

Inequality undermines the bonds of common and equal citizenship. These are built on a shared recognition of equal worth, the core principle of equality, but such recognition is impeded where rich and poor inhabit different worlds. Wealth enables some people to segregate themselves off from the rest of society – symbolized in gated communities – and to exclude themselves from the common institutions of society, notably education, health and public transport. The wealthy are therefore less likely to recognize the common citizenship of people living in poverty (or even the existence of poverty) and their own responsibilities as citizens towards them. Their support for social citizenship rights, both benefits and services, is likely to be weak if they regard them as of no relevance to their own lives. By the same token socioeconomic inequality is inimical to genuine equal political citizenship. Inequalities of economic resources translate into inequalities of power and influence as do cross-cutting inequalities such as gender, ethnicity and disability.

Equality also acts as the cement of social solidarity and cohesion. In the same way that inequality undermines common citizenship so it weakens social solidarity and cohesion. It is much harder to feel a sense of social solidarity with someone you consider inferior to yourself than with someone you regard as your equal. Social cohesion is part of the nexus of factors identified by Wilkinson and Pickett as linking inequality with ill-health and a range of other social problems such as violence.[9] Their analysis has been particularly significant in highlighting the impact of inequality on individuals and the fabric of their social relationships. The key factor here is the psychosocial stresses created by social status differentials. Recognition as a fellow human being worthy of respect has been identified as a basic human need. It is not surprising therefore that disrespect, humiliation and stigma through a process of 'othering' are, according to Wilkinson and Pickett, harmful to the mental and physical health of those at the bottom of an unequal socioeconomic hierarchy. Arguably the hatred shown to some minority groups, most recently disabled people, is likely to have similarly harmful effects.

Conversely, a more equal society creates the conditions in which individuals are better able to flourish and achieve their potential and to pursue the kind of life that will bring them satisfaction and meaning. Anti-egalitarians confuse equality with uniformity when they argue the opposite. And they fail to understand the ways in which greater equality strengthens positive liberty: the freedom to live the life one wants to live (a similar notion to the capabilities approach mentioned earlier). Inequality also fuels the rampant materialism that, far from enhancing liberty and diversity, fetters and diminishes our lives, creates impossible choices for those without the money to enjoy the baubles of conspicuous consumption dangled before their eyes and threatens to destroy the planet.

ADVANCING EQUALITY

Any strategy to create a more equal society will need to combine redistribution of income and wealth with pre-distribution (the term increasingly used to refer to the original distribution of earnings). There is growing interest in pre-distribution in recognition of the fact that greater equality cannot be achieved through redistribution through the tax-benefit system alone. Decent wages at the bottom and some form of restraint on obscenely high rewards at the top are required. They should be underpinned by a public debate about the value we attach to different kinds of work, which is a highly gendered question.

With regard to redistribution, even the OECD has acknowledged its importance in combating growing inequality. Labour now needs to show more courage in making the case for progressive taxation of income and wealth and for decent benefits than it did during the Blair-Brown years. Redistribution by stealth, while at the same time disparaging the idea of redistribution and talking tough about benefit claimants, did nothing to gain the kind of public support needed to build on the progressive measures that New Labour did take. Indeed, some analysts have suggested that New Labour's stance had the opposite effect of contributing to the significant weakening in support for redistribution among the general public.

The current anti-redistributive mood should not, though, be used as an excuse for inaction. Public attitudes are not fixed and the British Social Attitudes Survey indicates that a significant proportion of the public are potentially open to persuasion. Moreover, there is a long-standing widely held belief that the income gap is far too wide (even while it is typically massively underestimated). In the wake of the economic crisis and stagnating living standards for the majority, the damaging impact of inequality has been in the spotlight like never before, from the direct action of the Occupy movement to the leader columns of the *Financial Times*. This represents a potential sea change in politics of the kind identified by James Callaghan back in 1979. Labour must seize the moment and fashion a vision of a more equal social democratic society capable of inspiring the necessary support for the radical policies required to achieve it.

NOTES

1. J. Hills et. al., *An Anatomy of Economic Inequality in the UK*, London: Government Equalities Office, 2010
2. The Fabian Commission on Life Chances and Child Poverty, *Narrowing the Gap*, London: Fabian Society, 2006
3. P. Diamond and A. Giddens, 'The New Egalitarianism: Economic Inequality in the UK' in A. Giddens and P. Diamond (eds.) *The New Egalitarianism*, Cambridge: Polity Press, 2005; pp.108 and 100
4. M.C. Nussbaum and A. Sen (eds) *The Quality of Life*, Oxford: Clarendon Press, 1993
5. A. Giddens, *Where Now for New Labour?* Cambridge: Polity Press, 2002
6. P. Diamond, 'Empowerment and Transparency: A New Settlement for Public Services' and L. Byrne 'Eliminating "Power Failures": A New Agenda for Tackling Inequality' in R. Philpot (ed.) *The Purple Book: A Progressive Future for Labour,* London: Biteback, 2011
7. M. Glasman, 'Labour as a Radical Tradition' in M. Glasman, J. Rutherford, M. Stears and S. White (eds.) *The Labour Tradition and the Politics of Paradox*, LW Online Books, 2011; pp.14 and 27
8. L. Bamfield and T. Horton, *Understanding Attitudes to Tackling Economic Inequality*, London: Joseph Rowntree Foundation, 2009; T. Lanning and K. Lawton, *Getting What We Deserve?* London: IPPR, 2011
9. R. Wilkinson and K. Pickett, *The Spirit Level*, London: Penguin, 2010. See also, K. Rowlingson and S. McKay, *Wealth and the Wealthy*, Bristol: The Policy Press, 2012; chapter 2

Chapter 7

BETTER TOGETHER

A New Vision for All Children

Lisa Nandy MP

A legacy for children and young people was one of the great success stories of the last Labour government. Over half a million children were lifted out of poverty through a combined effort led by national government through a national strategy, targets and funding, and delivered through local structures. The creation of a Department for Children, Schools and Families helped to drive change through government and push children's issues up the political agenda, and there was a clear focus on outcomes for children through the Every Child Matters framework. Taken together, these actions brought about dramatic improvements for many of the most disadvantaged children while ensuring wider benefits for children in general.

Since 2010 that wider support system around children and their families has been dismantled. Its deconstruction has drawn little attention in the face of sweeping reforms to the education system. The Secretary of State for Education, Michael Gove, came into office with a focus on education and a determination to get started. The Academies Act was the first flagship piece of legislation passed by the Coalition, rushed through the House of Commons in just a few days under powers normally reserved for terrorism legislation.

Since then Gove's reforms to the education system have attracted controversy. The establishment of free schools and academies, for example, broke up the local authority family of schools with the

stated aim of devolving power, but has met strong criticism for centralizing power in the hands of the Secretary of State, away from
local communities.

Meanwhile, the wider support system for children has been
stripped away. The Early Intervention Grant which funded Sure
Start and other initiatives, short breaks for disabled children, and
targeted help for disadvantaged young people were immediately cut
by 11% and have been cut again since. This has led over 100 Sure
Start Centres to close across the country. Local authority children's
services budgets have also seen above average reductions in spending
– in some areas by over 40%, with a particular impact on preventative services.[1] Youth services, which were a lifeline for some of the
most disadvantaged young people, have been reduced or in some
cases disappeared.[2] The President of the Association of Directors
of Children's Services, Matt Dunkley, described the impact of these
combined cuts as putting 'a whole generation at risk'.[3]

Focusing on what happens inside the classroom is undoubtedly
important and was a key plank of the last government's Every Child
Matters programme. But as Dunkley recognizes, what happens in
the classroom cannot, on its own, compensate for what happens outside it.

By 2015, with the wider support system for children largely
dismantled, there will be an urgent need to focus on the most disadvantaged children. The Institute for Fiscal Studies forecasts that
by 2015 child poverty will have risen to 2.9 million leaving nearly
one-quarter of all children growing up in poverty.[4] Teacher surveys
indicate children are increasingly coming to school too hungry to
learn, while 77% of social workers say their caseloads are unman-
ageable.[5] It is self-evident that children who arrive at school hungry,
tired and with unresolved problems will not perform well. While
charities have focused their efforts on dealing with this problem,
setting up food banks across the country, there is urgency to this
problem which requires government intervention.

Similarly some children lack the resources and confidence to reach
their potential. National initiatives which successfully addressed
this, such as the Education Maintenance Allowance and Aim Higher,
were abolished by the incoming government while wider issues, such
as the impact of poor housing on ability to learn have been ignored.
Michael Gove's approach – to strip away state support and focus

exclusively on what happens inside the classroom – inevitably leaves some children behind.

Reforms to the education system also threaten to leave some children further and further behind. Free schools have proven expensive – the amounts spent per pupil are well above average at a time when education spending is at its lowest level for nearly 50 years. This is of more concern because the first 24 free schools to be established were, according to market analysts CACI, populated by 'middle class suburban people'. This was a trend that also emerged in Sweden, which pioneered free schools and where, according to the Education Minister, they are 'generally attended by children of better education and wealthy families making things even more difficult for children attending ordinary schools in poor areas'.[6]

We know that greater inequality is bad for us all, not just the most disadvantaged. As Wilkinson and Pickett's book *The Spirit Level* so convincingly demonstrated, ensuring that the lowest performing children do well is good for all children.[7] One way of ensuring that, regardless of intake, children do not fall behind is to replace this competitive, market-driven model with a collaborative approach. The City Challenge programme was an example of how schools working together to share expertise and resources could help to lift the achievement of all children. The state provided the framework, and the schools provided the expertise and energy to make it succeed.

Similarly, the narrowing of the curriculum and the introduction of the English Baccalaureate which forces schools to focus on five core academic subjects threatens to exclude many children. According to the Education Select Committee a 'focus on a fairly narrow range of subjects, demanding considerable curriculum time, is likely to have negative consequences on the uptake of other subjects'.[8] Technical education is particularly important for the half of children who do not go on to university, and for the economy. Many of the jobs that schoolchildren will go on to do in the future have not yet been created, so a wider focus on creativity and resilience is important for them, and for us.

Most of all, so many of Gove's reforms fly in the face of international evidence about what works. The OECD's extensive research suggests that strong accountability, combined with autonomy is the most effective way to raise performance.[9] This suggests that local accountability matters more than league tables which can be manipulated. Schools are not islands, and should be part of and accountable to their local communities. International evidence also suggests that devolving power to classroom level is highly effective, as it gives teachers the ability to tailor their approach. One example of this might be teaching different age groups together, recognizing that children learn at different rates and that trying to make the system too rigid leaves some children behind.

Gove's vision for children is one where some children will fall further behind. There is a strong Labour tradition – that introduced child benefit, that established a Department for Children to ensure that children were visible in public policy decisions which affect them and that provided strong support outside the classroom as well as in it – which is both distinctly different from this, and which understands that without a national vision for all children and young people – delivered locally – society will be profoundly poorer.

NOTES

1. NSPCC and CIPFA report, *Smart Cuts? Public Spending on Children's Social Care*, 2011
2. Education Select Committee, *Services for Young People*, 15 June 2011
3. See P. Butler, 'Cuts putting a whole generation at risk', *Guardian*, 30 March 2011
4. IFS and Joseph Rowntree Foundation, *Child and Working Age Poverty from 2010–2020*, 2011
5. British Association of Social Work, *State of Social Work*, March 2012
6. L. Nandy, 'Why Labour Should Not Embrace Free Schools', *New Statesman*, 18 April 2011
7. R. Wilkinson and K. Pickett, *The Spirit Level: Why Equality is Better for Everyone*, London: Allen Lane, 2010
8. Education Select Committee, *The English Baccalaureate*, 19 July 2011
9. OECD PISA study: www.oecd.org/pisa

Chapter 8

A ONE NATION APPROACH TO HEALTH AND SOCIAL CARE

Andy Burnham MP

For the first time in 20 years, our party has the chance to rethink its health and care policy from first principles. Whatever your political views, it's a big moment.

It presents the chance to change the terms of the health and care debate. For too long, it has been trapped on narrow ground, in technical debates about regulation, commissioning and competition. It is struggling to come up with credible answers to the questions that the twenty-first century is asking with ever-greater urgency.

I want to change the debate by opening up new possibilities and posing new questions of my own, starting with people and families and what they want.

Everything I say is based on two unshakable assumptions. First, that health and care will need to be delivered in a tighter fiscal climate for the foreseeable future, so we have to think even more fundamentally about getting better results for people and families from what we already have. Second, our fragile NHS has no capacity for further top-down reorganization, having been ground down by the current round. I know that any changes must be delivered through the organizations and structures we inherit in 2015. But that can't mean planning for no change. Those questions that the twenty-first century is bringing demand answers.

When modern conditions mean we are all living with higher levels of stress, change and insecurity, how do we give families the mental health support they need but remove the stigma? How will we ensure we are not overwhelmed by the costs of treating diseases linked to lifestyle and diet? And how can we stop people fearing old age to instead have true peace of mind throughout a longer life? These are huge questions that require scale and a sense of ambition in our answers.

When a Labour opposition last undertook this exercise, the world looked very different. But it had to be similarly ambitious. People were waiting months and years for hospital treatment, even dying on NHS waiting lists. So Labour set itself the mission of rescuing a beleaguered NHS which was starting to look as if it was on the way out. A big ambition and, by and large, with the help of the professions, we succeeded. We left office with waiting lists at an all-time low and patient satisfaction at an all-time high; a major turnaround from the NHS we inherited in 1997.

But that doesn't tell the whole story. I can trace the moment that made me think differently, and challenge an approach that was too focused on hospitals. In early 2007, my sister-in-law was in the Royal Marsden dying from breast cancer. After visiting one night, she called me over and asked if I could get her home to be with her four children. I told her I thought I could. But, after a day of phone calls, I will never forget having to go back to Claire and say it couldn't be done. As a government, we were talking about choice. But we were unable to respond to the most fundamental and meaningful choices people wanted to make.

Concerns about the way we care for people in the later stages of life, as well as how it is paid for, have built and built over the last decade. Stories of older people neglected or abused in care homes, isolated in their own homes or lost in acute hospitals – disorientated and dehydrated – recurred with ever-greater frequency. I have thought long and hard about why this is happening.

It is in part explained by regulatory failures; changes in professional practice – including nurse training – may also have played a part. But, in my view, these explanations deal with the symptoms rather than the cause of a problem that goes much deeper.

My penny-drop moment came last year when I was work-shadowing a ward sister at the Royal Derby. It was not long after the Prime

Minister had proposed hourly bed rounds for nurses. I asked her what she thought of that. Her answer made an impression on me.

It was not that nurses didn't care any more, she said. On the whole, they did. It was more that the wards today are simply not staffed to deal with the complexity of what the ageing society is bringing to them. When she qualified, it was rare to see someone in their 80s on the ward after a major operation. Now there are ever-greater numbers of very frail people in their 80s and 90s, with intensive physical, mental and social care needs. Hospitals hadn't changed to reflect this new reality, she said, and nurses were struggling to cope with it.

They were still operating on a twentieth-century production-line model, with a tendency to see the immediate problem – the broken hip, the stroke – but not the whole person behind it. They are geared up to meet physical needs, but not provide the mental or social support that we will all need in the later stages of life. So our hospitals, designed for the last century, are in danger of being overwhelmed by the demographic challenges of this.

And that is the crux of our problem.

To understand its roots, it helps to go back to the 1948 World Health Organization definition of health: 'a state of complete physical, mental and social well-being and not merely the absence of disease or infirmity.' A simple vision which stands today.

But, for all its strengths, the NHS was not set up to achieve it. It went two-thirds of the way, although mental health was not given proper priority, but the third, social, was left out altogether. The trouble is that 'social' is the preventative part. Helping people with daily living, staying active and independent, delays the day they need more expensive physical and mental support. But deep in the DNA of the NHS is the notion that the home, the place where so much happens to affect health, is not its responsibility. It doesn't pay for grab rails or walk-in showers, even if it is accepted that they can keep people safer and healthy.

The exclusion of the social side of care from the NHS settlement explains why it has never been able to break out of a 'treatment service' mentality and truly embrace prevention. It is a medical model; patient-centred, not person-centred.

But, in reality, it's even worse than that. For 65 years, Britain has tried to meet one person's needs not through two but three services: physical, through the mainstream NHS; mental, through a detached system on the fringes of the NHS; and social, through a means-tested and charged-for council service that varies greatly from one area to the next.

One person. Three care services.

For most of the twentieth century, we just about managed to make it work for most people. When people had chronic or terminal illness at a younger age, they could still cope with daily living even towards the end of life. Families lived closer to each other and, with a bit of council support, could cope.

Now, in the century of the ageing society, the gaps between our three services are getting dangerous. The twenty-first century is asking questions of our twentieth-century health and care system that, in its current position, it will never be able to answer to the public's satisfaction.

As we live longer, people's needs become a blur of the physical, mental and social. It is just not possible to disaggregate them and meet them through our three separate services. But that's what we're still trying to do. So, wherever people are in this disjointed system, some or all of one person's needs will be left unmet. In the acute hospital ward, social and mental needs can be neglected. This explains why older people often go downhill quickly on admission to hospital. In mental health care settings, people can have their physical health overlooked, in part explaining why those with serious mental health problems die 15 years younger than the rest of the population. And, in places, such is the low standard of social care provision in both the home and care homes that barely any needs are properly met. What, realistically, can be achieved from a home care service based around ten-minute slots per person?

On a practical level, families are looking for things from the current system that it just isn't able to provide. They desperately want co-ordination of care – a single point of contact for all of mum or dad's needs – but it's unlikely to be on offer in a three-service world.

So people continue to face the frustration of telling the same story over again to all of the different council and NHS professionals who come through the door. Carers get ground down by the battle to get support, spending days on the phone being passed from pillar to post.

So far, I have spoken about the experience of older people and their carers. But the problems I describe – the lack of a whole-person approach – holds equally true for the start of life. Parents of children with severe disabilities will recognize the pattern – the battle for support, the lack of co-ordination and a single point of contact. CAMHS[1] support at the right time can make all the difference to a young life but is often not there when it is needed. Children on the autistic spectrum are frequently missed altogether. The mantra is that early intervention makes all the difference. But it is rarely a reality in a system that doesn't have prevention at its heart.

If we leave things as they are, carers of young and old will continue to feel the frustration of dealing with services which don't provide what they really need, that don't see the whole person or the whole child. They won't provide the quality people want. But nor will they be financially sustainable in this century.

Right now, the incentives are working in the wrong direction. For older people, the gravitational pull is towards hospital and care home. For the want of spending a few hundred pounds in the home, we seem to be happy to pick up hospital bills for thousands.

We are paying for failure on a grand scale, allowing people to fail at home and drift into expensive hospital beds and from there into expensive care homes. The trouble is no one has the incentive to invest in prevention. Councils face different pressures and priorities than the NHS, with significant cuts in funding and an overriding incentive to keep council tax low. So care services have been whittled away, in the knowledge that the NHS will always provide a safety net for people who can't cope. And, of course, this could be said to suit hospitals as they get paid for each person who comes through the door.

In their defence, councils and the NHS may be following the institutional logic of the systems they are in. But it's financial madness, as well as being bad for people. Hospital chief executives tell me that, on any given day, around 30–40% of beds are occupied by older people who, if better provision was available, would not need to be there. If we leave things as they are, our District General Hospitals will be like warehouses of older people – lined up on the wards because we failed to do something better for them. But it gets worse. Once they are there, they go downhill for lack of whole-person support and end up on a fast-track to care homes – costing them and us even more.

We could get much better results for people, and much more for the money we spend on the NHS and on social care, but only if we turn this system on its head. We need incentives in the right place – keeping people at home and out of hospitals. We must take away the debates between different parts of the public sector, where the NHS won't invest if councils reap the benefit and vice versa, that are utterly meaningless to the public.

So the question I have put at the heart of Labour's policy review is this: is it time for the full integration of health and social care?

One budget, one service co-ordinating all of one person's needs: physical, mental and social. Whole-Person Care. A service that starts with what people want – to stay comfortable at home – and is built around them. When you start to think of a one-budget, one-service world, all kinds of new possibilities open up. If the NHS was commissioned to provide Whole-Person Care in all settings – physical, mental, social from home to hospital – a decisive shift can be made towards prevention.

A year-of-care approach to funding, for instance, would finally put the financial incentives where they need to be. NHS hospitals would be paid more for keeping people comfortable at home rather than admitting them. That would be true human progress in the century of the ageing society. Commissioning acute trusts in this way could change the terms of the debate about hospitals at a stroke. Rather than feeling under constant siege, it could create positive conditions for the District General Hospital to evolve over time into a fundamentally different entity: an integrated care provider from home to hospital.

In Torbay, where the NHS and council have already gone some way down this path, around 200 beds have been taken out from the local hospital without any great argument, as families have other things they truly value: unlike other parts of England, they have one point of contact for the co-ordination of health and care needs. Occupational therapists visit homes the same day or the day after they are requested; urgent aids and adaptations are supplied in minutes not days. If an older person has to go into hospital, a care worker provides support on the ward, and ensures the right package of care is in place to help get them back home as soon as possible. Imagine what a step forward it would be if we could introduce these three things across England.

For the increasing numbers of people who are filled with dread at the thought of mum or dad going into hospital, social care support on the ward would provide instant reassurance. It is a clear illustration of what becomes possible in a one-service, one-budget world with prevention at its heart.

If local hospitals are to grow into integrated providers of Whole-Person Care, then it will make sense to continue to separate general care from specialist care, and to continue to centralize the latter. So hospitals will need to change and we shouldn't fear that. But, with the change I propose, we can also put that whole debate on much a better footing.

If people accept changes to some parts of the local hospital, it becomes more possible to protect the parts that they truly value – specifically local general acute and emergency provision.

The model I am proposing could create a firmer financial base under acute hospitals trusts where they can sustain a back-stop, local A&E service as part of a more streamlined, remodelled, efficient local health-care system. So A&Es need not close for purely or pre-dominantly financial reasons, although a compelling clinical case for change must always be heard.

I am clear that we will never make the most of our £120 billion health and care budget unless hospitals have positive reasons to grow into the community, and we break down the divide between primary and secondary care.

It could see GPs working differently, as we can see in Torbay, leading teams of others professionals – physios, occupational therapists, district nurses – managing the care of the at-risk older population.

Nerves about hospital takeover start to disappear in a one-budget world where the financial incentives work in the opposite direction. NHS hospitals need the security to embrace change and that change will happen more quickly in an NHS Preferred Provider world rather than an Any Qualified Provider (AQP) world, where every change is an open tender.

I don't shy away from saying this. I believe passionately in the public NHS and what it represents. I think a majority of the public share this sentiment. They are uncomfortable with mixing medi-cine with the money motive. They support what the NHS represents – people before profits – as memorably celebrated by Danny Boyle at the opening ceremony of the Olympic Games. Over time, allow-ing the advance of a market with no limits will undermine the core, emergency, public provision that people hold dear.

So I challenge those who say that the continued advance of comp-etition and the market into the NHS is the answer to the challenges of this century. The evidence simply doesn't support it – financially or on quality grounds. If we look around the world, market-based health systems cost more per person not less than the NHS. The planned nature of our system, under attack from the current government's reforms, is its most precious strength in facing a century when demand will ratchet up. Rather than allowing the NHS model to be gradually eroded, we should be protecting it and extending it as the most efficient way of meeting this century's pressures.

The AQP approach will not deliver what people want either. Families are demanding integration. Markets deliver fragmentation. The logical conclusion of the open-tender approach is to bring in an ever-increasing number of providers on to the pitch, dealing with ever-smaller elements of a person's care, without an overall co-ordinating force. If we look to the USA, the best providers are working on that highly integrated basis, co-ordinating physical, mental and social care from home to hospital. We have got to take the best of that approach and universalize it.

But there are dangers of monopolistic or unresponsive providers. Even if the NHS is co-ordinating all care, it is essential that people are able to choose other providers. And within a managed system there must always be a role for the private and voluntary sectors and the innovation they bring. But let me say something that the last Labour government didn't make clear: choice is not the same thing as competition. The system I am describing will only work if it is based around what people and families want, giving them full control. To make that a reality we want to empower patients to have more control over their care, such as dialysis treatment in the home or the choice to die at home or in a hospice. We will work towards extending patients rights to treatment in the NHS constitution. The system would have to change to provide what people want, rather than vice versa.

The best advert for the people-centred system in Torbay is that more people there than in any other part of England die at home. When I visited, they explained that they had never set out to achieve that – a target had not been set – but it had been a natural consequence of a system built around people. A real lesson there for politicians. So an NHS providing all care – physical, mental and social – would be held to account by powerful patient rights.

But, as part of our consultation, we will be asking whether it follows that local government could take a prominent role working in partnership with Clinical Commissioning Groups (CCGs) on commissioning with a single budget. This change would allow a much more ambitious approach to commissioning than we have previously managed. At the moment, we are commissioning health services. This was the case with Primary Care Trusts (PCTs) and will remain so with CCGs.

The challenges of the twenty-first century are such that we need to make a shift to commissioning for good population health, making the link with housing, planning, employment, leisure and education. This approach to commissioning, particularly in the early years, begins to make the Marmot vision a reality, where all the determinants of health are in play.[2]

But it also solves a problem that is becoming increasingly urgent. Councils are warning that, within a decade, they will be overwhelmed by the costs of care if nothing changes. They point to a chart – affectionately known as the 'graph of doom' – which shows there will be little money for libraries, parks and leisure centres in 2020. One of the great strengths of the one-budget, whole-person approach would be to break this downward spiral. It would give local government a positive future and local communities a real say. The challenge becomes not how to patch two conflicting worlds together but how to make the most of a single budget.

To address fears that health money will be siphoned off into other, unrelated areas, reassurance is provided by a much more clearly defined national entitlement, based around a strengthened National Institute for Health and Care Excellence (NICE), able to take a broader view of all local public spending when making its recommendations.

It won't be the job of people at local level to decide *what* should be provided. That will be set out in a new entitlement. But it will be their job to decide *how* it should be provided. That would provide clarity about the respective roles of national and local government, too often a source of confusion and tension.

But let me be clear: nothing I have said today requires a top-down structural reorganization. In the same way that Andrew Lansley should have refocused PCTs and put doctors in charge, I will simply refocus the organizations I inherit to deliver this vision of Whole-Person Care. The Health and Well-Being Board could come to the fore, with CCGs supporting them with technical advice. While we retain the organizations, we will repeal the Health and Social Care Act 2012 and the rules of the market. It is a confused, sub-optimal piece of legislation, not worthy of the NHS and which fails to give the clarity respective bodies need about their role. This approach creates the conditions for the evolutionary change towards the whole-person vision rather than structural upheaval.

At a stroke, those two crucial local institutions – council and hospital – have an alignment of interests and a clear future role to grow into.

But the same is true for social care. At present, it is trapped in a failing financial model. The great attraction of the whole-person approach, with the NHS taking responsibility for co-ordination, is that it will be in a position to raise the standards and horizons of social care, lifting it out of today's cut-price, minimum-wage business. Social care carers would be more valued and young people would be able to progress as part of an integrated whole-person Care workforce.

So 'Whole-Person Care' is the proposal at the heart of Labour's health and care policy review led by Liz Kendall.

The fact is that, even if we move to a fully integrated model, and shift resources from hospital to home, it won't be enough to pay for all of one person's care needs. We need to be very clear about that. So this opens up the question of the funding of social care. It is the case that, with the shift of resources out of hospital, more preventative social care could be provided in the home and, in all likelihood, better standards of social care offered, as we have seen in Torbay. For instance, we have already proposed that this should include people on the end-of-life register. It would also include provision for those with the highest needs and at risk from going into hospital.

But rather than leave this unspecified, people need to know exactly where they stand. Currently, council care provision is the ultimate lottery. In a single system, it would be right to set for the first time a clear entitlement to what social care could be provided on what terms, as part of a national entitlement to health and care. That would help people understand what is not covered – which is very unclear to people at present.

But the question arises: what is the fairest way of helping people cover the rest? At present, beyond the £23,000 floor, care charges are unlimited. These are 'dementia taxes'. The more vulnerable you are, the more you pay: as cruel as pre-NHS or US health care. No other part of our welfare state works in this way and, in the century of the ageing society, failure to resolve how we pay for care could undermine the NHS, the contributory principle and incentives to save. Some people might ask why they should save for retirement, when the chances of it all being washed away increase every year? In this century, we can't carry on letting people go into old age with everything – home, savings, pension – on the roulette table.

So there is a political consensus that the status quo is the worst of all possible worlds and it needs to change. We agree about the need to find a fairer way of paying for social care, but not on what that system should be. The government have begun to set out their version of Andrew Dilnot's proposals.[3] A cap, not of £35,000 but over the £50,000 Dilnot recommended, and possibly up to £75,000. For Labour, it fails a basic One Nation test. This is better than the status quo. But it also fails a sustainability test. By failing to address the shortfall in council budgets, it leaves people exposed to ever-increasing care charges and more likely to pay up to the level of the cap. To many this won't feel like progress.

So, as part of Labour's policy consultation, we will ask for views on other ways of paying for social care. We will only have a solution when all people, regardless of their savings and the severity of their needs, have the chance to protect what they have worked for. There are two basic choices – a voluntary or all-in approach – and, at this stage, we are seeking views on which path people think we should take, building on the foundations of a fully merged health and social care system. Both would represent a significant improvement on the status quo, but both present significant difficulties in terms of implementation. Andrew Dilnot's proposed cap and means-test would help everyone protect their savings. It would mean people only pay as much as they need to, but, in the worst case scenario, could stand to lose a significant chunk of their savings.

One of the problems with the voluntary approach is it assumes the continuation of two care worlds – one charged for, the other one free-at-the-point-of-use – with all its complexity. So it is right to ask whether we can move to an all-in system, and extend the NHS principle to all care. This would mean asking people to pay differently for social care to create a level playing field on how all care is provided. But it would only work on the all-in principle and that is its major downside: all people would be required to contribute, rather than just those needing care. People's exposure to care costs in an all-in system would be significantly lower. But, as with any insurance system, people might pay and never end up using the service.

It is an open question whether a broad consensus can be found on funding social care on either a voluntary or all-in principle.

But Labour is clear that this must not stand in the way of progress now to get much more for people from what we currently spend on health and care.

To Beveridge's five giants of the twentieth century (want, disease, ignorance, squalor and idleness), the twenty-first is rapidly adding a sixth: fear of old age. If we do nothing, that fear will only grow as we hear more and more stories of older people failed by a system that is simply not geared up to meet their needs.

A One Nation approach to health and care means giving all people freedom from this fear, all families peace of mind.

Whole-Person Care is a vision for a truly integrated service, not just battling disease and infirmity but able to aspire to give all people a complete state of physical, mental and social well-being. It is a people-centred service which starts with people's lives, their hopes and dreams, and builds out from there, strengthening and extending the NHS in the twenty-first century, not whittling it away. It is a service which affords everyone's parents the dignity and respect we would want for our own. The task is urgent because the NHS is on the same fast-track to fragmentation that social care has been down. The further it carries on down this path, the harder it will be to glue it back together. Unlike the last general election, the next one needs to give people a proper choice of what kind of health and care system they want in the twenty-first century.

That's why I started by saying it's time to change the terms of the debate and put more ambition into our ideas. Labour is rediscovering its roots and its ability to think in the boldest terms about a society that cares for everyone and leaves no one behind. People need One Nation Labour to be as brave in this century as Bevan was in the last. That is the challenge and we will rise to it.

NOTES

1. Child and Adolescent Mental Health Service
2. M. Marmot, *Fair Society, Healthy Lives*, London: UCL, 2011
3. Commission on Funding of Care Report, 2011

Chapter 9

PUBLIC SECTOR REFORM AND SOCIAL DEMOCRACY

Raymond Plant

The distinction between means and ends has been absolutely central to social democracy since its nineteenth-century inception and at various times debates about this issue have been central to Labour Party politics. This was particularly true in the 1950s when there was a major debate about the role of nationalization linked to the possible removal of Clause 4 from the Labour Party's constitution. The debate then was about whether public ownership was one of the goals or ends of democratic socialism, or whether it was an indispensable means, or just one of a number of different means of attaining democratic socialist ends such as liberty, equality and fraternity or greater social solidarity. This was essentially what was called the revisionist approach to democratic socialism/social democracy – that ends were fundamental but that there was a need to be open-minded and empirical about the appropriate means to achieve these ends.

This debate was also central to arguments over the Third Way and Blairism. Tony Blair was clear that there are certain fundamental values definitive of social democracy which do not change, coupled with the idea that many of Labour's traditional means for attaining these goals were now to be regarded as outdated and ineffective. This was particularly true of the role of the public sector in the pursuit of social democratic goals. Blairism challenged the traditional Labour attitude that the combination of state funding and state provision of public services was a necessary condition for attaining these fundamental values. However, Blairite critics argued that such forms of provision had in fact created rather monolithic forms of service which were not sufficiently sensitive to the needs and aspirations of people. Moreover, state funding and state provision had led to the establishment of substantial producer interest groups in the public sector which were resistant to change and which also tended to defend forms of service delivery which were in the interests of the producers rather than those who consumed them. They had also done little or nothing to overcome inequality which was, from a Labour perspective, supposed to be one of the important aims of public provision. One of the social democratic aims for public provision was that publicly funded and provided institutions and services would ensure standards of services which would diminish inequality by removing the incentive to choose private forms of provision in health and education particularly. This, however, had not occurred and both public/independent schools were in fact flourishing as was private medicine.

So, central to the more radical side of Blairism was the idea that the state could and should retain the function of funding public services and making clear the strategic objectives and priorities of these services while at the same time creating the opportunity for a wide variety of institutions: state, social enterprises, for profit firms, and the voluntary sector to actually bid for contracts from the state to provide services. This competition for state funding on the part of providers would increase efficiency and lead to services being designed much more with the consumer in mind. It would allow for the greater personalization of services, respond much more to consumer choice and be generally more flexible and innovative in the provision of services. The development of such features which were inhibited by public provision, although not by public funding, were essential to meeting people's aspirations which otherwise would be pursued in the private sector. The argument was that social democratic ends could be achieved by a diversity of means so long as central government retained the funding role and the strategic goal-setting role. On such a view, what has sometimes been called the contractual state is in fact wholly compatible with social democratic ends. Those who resisted these views were thought to be conservative defenders of vested interests, clinging to outmoded means of delivering agreed goals. If social democracy is always a revisionist creed – not revising goals but being continually open, empirical and non-ideological about means – then it was centrally important to ensure that the means of delivering agreed goals and purposes were to be examined dispassionately and empirically. So on this view a Third Way Blairite approach to the public sector, given that the goals were not being revised, was wholly compatible with the revisionist tradition of British social democracy. This can be seen by considering C.A.R. Crosland's *The Future of Socialism* published in 1956 in which he argues in Chapter 7 that there will be a growing demand for the personalization of services, which will be a demand difficult to meet via bureaucratically provided services that tend to think about public services in terms of broad categories of people and problems.[1] These more personalized needs are partly the result of the growth of individualism, partly the result of demographic trends in which people had lost traditional forms of family and community support. The government had to provide some kind of collective response to these problems, but Crosland was clear that this did not always mean state provision and he asked his readers to remember that the socialist tradition had an anarchical streak in it, which meant that the democratic socialist/social democrat did not always have to prefer the state over the individual. So, if we are to be revisionists in our day we have to take an analytical, empirical and critical view about what sorts of means will facilitate the achievement of social democratic ends and not to go directly to the default position that state provision, as well as state funding, is the only model compatible with social democratic goals.

The Blairite approach to provision has been enthusiastically extended by the Coalition in respect of the NHS reforms, Academy and free schools, and the involvement of voluntary and private sector providers in the delivery of various social security and benefit programmes. The difference is that while the contractual state is being vastly extended it is not in the service of social democratic goals and, perhaps most particularly, not of the goals of equality and fraternity or solidarity. It has, for example, been central to social democratic arguments about both comprehensive education and the NHS that these are indispensable means to these ends, not just one set of means among others: that a high-quality, comprehensive health service and comprehensive educational system would be part of creating a more equal society, one in which people shared the same kinds of experience in education and health and that this would lead to more social equality and to a more integrated society. So one issue that faces

Labour now is how far – both in reaction to what the Coalition is doing and in respect of its own policy making – it wishes to embrace a kind of pluralism of delivery, while ensuring that goals are still met by strategic goal setting, and how far it wants in fact to reverse current trends both in education, where nearly 50% of schools are now Academies, and in health where Labour has promised to reverse the participation of other 'willing providers' in the provision of health services. That is to say, the question is: are state-provided services as well as state funding indispensable for the delivery of social democratic values or is it possible to think that these values can be served equally well by a plurality of forms of provision, including for profit forms of providing services?

To some extent this depends on how we are to understand the goals or ends that influence which means we regard as being required or not. A good deal of the 1950s debates were, I think, a bit naive in that it was assumed that there was a set of settled ends – liberty, equality, fraternity – and that given these one could be entirely empirical about the means. So, for example, would more nationalization enhance the possibility of attaining these goals? But of course the goals are not all that clear cut and unambiguous – a point which I have discussed at length elsewhere.[2] But for the purposes of this chapter let us take just three examples of the complexity of the goals and how these will affect means. In the case of freedom it is crucial to understand whether we see liberty negatively, as the absence of coercion, in which case it is created by the rule of law, which secures as far as possible equal freedom from coercion together with police forces and legal institutions which sustain this. Or is freedom to be understood not just as freedom from but also freedom to – that is to say, freedom including ability, capability and power? If this is what freedom means, a free society will be one which certainly protects people from coercion but will also be about securing to individuals the resources necessary to pursue whatever their freely chosen goals are. Typically this means the provision of public services which secure to people the generic goods of health, education and welfare without which they would not be able to pursue any goals at all. Assuming that this second version of freedom is the more typically social democratic one how does this then relate to equality? In his book *Choose Freedom* Roy Hattersley provides a sophisticated and quintessentially social democratic response to this in his argument (which he credits to C.A.R. Crosland) that greater social and economic equality is needed as an essential instrument for securing more equal liberty in the positive sense of freedom (which it certainly would not for securing equal negative liberty).[3] For Hattersley, equality is essentially about greater equality of condition in the pursuit of freedom in this expanded sense. However, the more modern social democratic position associated with Blair and Brown has tended on the whole to favour equality of opportunity rather than greater equality of condition. In a sense this has to weaken the relationship between the essentially liberal democratic idea of equal freedom and equality more generally. For a social democrat like Hattersley, equality is an instrumental value; it is instrumental to achieving the highest degree of equal liberty in the positive sense. For the more modern social democrat with the emphasis on equality of opportunity there has to be a weaker link between liberty and equality because the emphasis on equality of opportunity, or the opportunity to become unequal, means that if we link this view of equality with positive freedom then the social democratic ideal would be that some people should become more free than others. If freedom is about ability, power and resources then high degrees of inequality as a result of a policy of equality of opportunity alone will mean an endorsement of the idea that in a social democratic society it is acceptable for some to have greater freedom than others.

I have not mentioned fraternity or solidarity partly because, as Steven Haseler argues in *The Gaitskellites*, the social democratic movement has embraced this value without quite knowing what to do with it or about it.[4] It is very difficult to make greater social solidarity a direct object of policy. Perhaps the most that can be done is to hope/expect that it will be a kind of by-product of other policies which create the opportunity for shared experiences, as in a comprehensive educational system and the NHS.

So my point is that the distinction between means and ends is by no means as straightforward as it seems. The ends in question are complex and, depending on which element in a complex value is being emphasized, the policy prescriptions may differ in quite fundamental ways. Also, even among the goals of social democracy one can be subordinated to another, so as in Hattersley's case greater equality of condition is needed to underpin choosing freedom, as the basic social democratic goal implies.

These rather theoretical points do have direct policy salience. Take two examples. The first is how a Labour government might handle arguments about welfare dependency. These have become important in modern debates about welfare. There is one response to this typical on the Left which seems to me to miss the point altogether. This is to respond to the argument about welfare dependency by arguing that we are all in one way or another dependent on other people, on institutions and communities of all sorts and therefore there is nothing specifically wrong with welfare dependency, which should give rise to concerns. This misses the point about welfare dependency, which is that the recipient of welfare is in fact dependent upon one source, namely one agency, and that this source has a high degree of discretion about how to deal with particular individuals so that the recipient of welfare may be on the sharp end of the exercise of monopoly and discretionary power. If this is seen as a serious problem, as I think that it is, then the argument about a distinction between funding and provision becomes important. If the state contracts with a range of providers then the client will have a range of alternative providers of the service, whatever it is, to choose from and will no longer be dependent upon just one provider.

Here an emphasis on liberty among social democratic values might well favour such an approach and a revisionist certainly cannot dismiss the argument out of hand. On the other hand, it might be argued that other values would be undermined by such an approach. So, for example, it might be argued that the funding/provider split in fact treats the citizen as being a consumer only looking to services to meet his or her own desire for autonomy and choice; whereas social democracy is about a significant degree of solidarity and common citizenship which is threatened by a consumerist approach to welfare provision. One way of putting the point is that there is at the very least a tension between liberty on the one hand and fraternity on the other. On the former view, liberty would favour diversity in provision with commonality of funding via the state and would see the funding as being itself the embodiment of solidarity and common citizenship. On this view the state does assume a communal responsibility via funding which can then be met in different ways by various providers and in so doing helps to increase freedom and choice. On the latter view, common citizenship and solidarity has to be delivered in terms of common provision as well as common funding. It would then on a revisionist view, have to be an empirical matter as to how far participation in the institutions of the welfare state does in fact encourage a sense of solidarity, common experience and a common culture. It would be very surprising if the same answer could be given about all forms of state provision ranging from hospitals, comprehensive schools and benefit offices – but it would be an empirical matter not a conceptual one and, if one is being a revisionist, not an ideological one either.

It might be argued that these distinctions are far too sharp because there might be ways in which state funding through a variety of providers could be modified to ensure a greater sense of common citizenship rather than just through state funding. There might well be two approaches here which would be worth considering. The first would be to increase community and user involvement in the management of those bodies whether social enterprises, for profit businesses or voluntary sector bodies so that a wider set of concerns could be represented in the management of such enterprises rather than just the imperatives of the enterprises themselves. Such representation could play a major role in ensuring that these requirements could either be written into the contracts between the funder and the provider or made a condition of being a recognized contractor. So, for example, it could become part of the condition of being a contractor that the commissioning body – whether central government, local government or an arms-length body – should require that the operation of the contract as well as being concerned with efficiency and effectiveness should also require that the contractor has to develop mechanisms to ensure equality of access to services and that these should be monitored. So under the Coalition the Secretary of State for Health has issued a detailed mandate to the NHS Commissioning Board to ensure that its commissioning practices should reflect governmental priorities for the service. There is no reason to think that a Labour secretary of state should not equally insist that commissioning reflects a social democratic commitment to equality of access to whatever service is in question; that this will be monitored and that if necessary the commissioning body will ensure that remedial action is taken. On this basis the concern with equal freedom, equality and a sense of community could be reflected in a pervasive way through the contractual regime. What from a social democratic point of view is wrong in principle with that?

The second alternative would be to consider a role for the Human Rights Act (HRA). This applies to Public Authorities which have to act in terms of its provisions. A Public Authority is one which performs public functions. Given that providers of services will be contracting to perform public functions, many of which indeed are statutory, then there is a case for saying that the requirements of the HRA should apply to providers either directly or in terms of the requirements of the contract. Again, if we believe that the HRA embodies a set of common rights which we have as citizens, then the provisions of the Act could be used to ensure that these standards of citizenship are in fact embodied in the provisions made by a plurality of providers.

On this view community representation in the management of public sector contractors could ensure that the contract embodies social concerns and priorities, including equality of access and, where it makes sense, equality of provision. The user of a contract which embodies social concerns and priorities and the HRA would be a way of ensuring that liberty is protected by means of a plurality of providers so that individuals have some degree of choice, which might be denied in a monolithic form of provision, while at the same time ensuring that there was a sense of common citizenship through common rights and community involvement in the management of provision together with a concern for greater equality as a requirement on commissioning bodies. This would seem to me to be reasonable revisionist response to what Crosland saw as the inevitable growth of individualism and the aspirations which go with this while retaining the central social democratic vision of the role of the welfare state.

NOTES

1. C.A.R. Crosland, *The Future of Socialism*, London: Cape, 1956
2. See R. Plant, *The Neo-liberal State*, Oxford: Oxford University Press, 2010
3. R. Hattersley, *Choose Freedom*, London: Penguin, 1987
4. S. Haseler, *The Gaitskellites*, London: Macmillan, 1969

Chapter 10

WHERE NEXT FOR SOCIALIST SOCIAL POLICY?

Robert M. Page

This chapter will focus on some of the key issues facing the Labour Party as it contemplates its future strategy in relation to social policy. Since the pioneering changes introduced by the Attlee governments from 1945–51, Labour has found it increasingly difficult to articulate a clear and distinctive narrative in relation to the role and purpose of the welfare state. Should the welfare state be regarded as a practical means of shaving the rough edges off capitalism by providing citizens with limited security from market forces and opportunities for material advancement? Or should it be seen as having a much deeper role to play in creating a society in which solidarism and selflessness can flourish? As Jeremy Nuttall argues in his book *Psychological Socialism,* although the creation of a 'more caring, responsible and intelligent society' has always been 'a significant strand in Labour's thinking', this has generally been of an unsystematic kind.[1] In part this reflects a deep-rooted scepticism about the value of 'utopian' thinking within party circles. Moreover, those who talk about the 'good society' or the improvement of the individual are often portrayed as having a 'Puritan' mindset and a disdain for the pursuit of personal pleasure, which liberal-minded revisionists such as Gaitskell, Crosland and Jenkins saw as an essential feature of socialism. Even some of those most strongly committed to a socially transformative welfare strategy in the post-1945 era have acknowledged that Labour will sometimes need to opt for incremental rather than radical change if they wanted to avoid running too far ahead of public opinion with the consequent threat of diminished electoral support. In practice, this has resulted in a range of minor welfare reforms with limited sense of a broader purpose. It will be argued that while the importance of designing and implementing effective 'piecemeal' social policies should not be underestimated, it is important that such activity is undertaken with far more ambitious objectives in mind. The need for a long-term strategy of this kind is vital if Labour is to avoid being seen as a 'modernizing' party which consistently dilutes its ideals or narrows its transformative vision in order to disguise its accommodation with a neo-liberal-inspired economic and social agenda.

One of the major criticisms of the previous New Labour governments (1997–2010) was that they allowed themselves to be transfixed by the idea that the direction of social policy should always mirror public opinion rather than those of 'unworldly' idealists and scholars. For example, Labour MP Frank Field has continually argued that the best way to help the poorest citizens, given their lack of effective electoral clout, is to ensure that 'pro-poor' policies are designed in ways deemed legitimate by more prosperous citizens.[2] Certainly, New Labour could point to public opinion evidence that suggests more egalitarian forms of democratic socialist social policy fail to resonate with the public. For example, the latest national public attitudes survey reports that only one-third of citizens support the proposition that taxes should be increased to pay for better health, education and social benefits. In addition, just 19% of those surveyed believe that poverty results from social injustice compared to 26% who link such disadvantage to laziness or a lack of willpower.[3]

New Labour's desire to become a party which floating voters in middle England would regard as 'one of us' led them to argue for a 'principled' rapprochement with the market and for the development of more muscular approaches to those aspects of the welfare state which were regarded as 'problematic' such as various means-tested forms of financial support. In terms of the latter, this involved a firm rejection of what has been termed a 'moral' social strategy which would involve persuading a sceptical public of the legitimacy of providing support for those commonly regarded as 'undeserving'. Instead, it was decided to fashion a defensive welfare strategy that would challenge the 'deep' socialist view that a focus on individual 'flaws' should only be contemplated *after* the systemic failings of the economy and the organization of society had been rectified. Accordingly, a twin track 'populist' approach was developed by New Labour in which progressive adjustments were made to the tax and benefit system to support 'hard working' parents and their children and more demanding conditions were imposed on those deemed to be making insufficient effort to join the ranks of the financially independent.

New Labour's more responsive approach to the market led to a greater willingness to embrace revisionist welfare ideas promoted by Left-leaning commentators such as Julian Le Grand.[4] Rejecting the idea that any shortcomings of state welfare could be attributed to strategic oversights, inadequate resource levels, limited participatory mechanisms or demotivated staff, these revisionist 'socialists' sought to challenge the idea that egalitarian objectives could only be achieved by means of publicly funded *and* publicly provided services that operated within a distinctive set of ethical, non-commercial parameters. This led to a more technocratic, evidence-based form of policy making and the promotion of non-state and quasi market initiatives. One of the outcomes of this development was much less emphasis on the non-measurable, 'intangible' gains that arise from solidaristic- and altruistic-based procedures and practices. Over time this has led Labour to advocate particular policies, such as the creation of NHS Foundation Hospital Trusts, Academy schools or direct payment schemes for service users, on the basis of a narrow test of effectiveness (does it work?) rather than on broader 'ideological' considerations (is it socialist?). In charting the way ahead for social policy it is this latter perspective that needs to come to the fore. There will inevitably be heated discussions over whether one type of policy could be deemed more 'socialist' than another, but this is preferable to a situation in which there is little if any debate about the broader implications of continuing with a particular policy (free schools) or a significant policy shift (an increased role for voluntary sector welfare provision) on the grounds that such discussions would represent unnecessary distractions from the pressing issues of the day.

In order to highlight the difficulties faced by Labour in terms of its prospective social policy agenda, attention will be given to four interlinked dilemmas that a future Labour government will need to contemplate, namely: the individual or the community, centralism or localism, universalism or diversity, and public or non-public provision.

THE INDIVIDUAL OR THE COMMUNITY?

The question of whether socialist social policy should be designed in ways to create strong autonomous individuals as opposed to more solidarity-inclined citizens in which the collective good is prioritized remains a pertinent one for Labour as it has for other European social democrats.[5] Those in the former camp contend that the key role for social policy is to minimize the possibility that individuals will become beholden to their family, neighbours, or employers in charting their life course. Citizens should be able to rely on a benevolent welfare state to provide them with all necessary forms of support such as education, health care, and financial support to enable them to pursue a life course of their choosing, irrespective of 'chance' factors such as family background and social class. In contrast, communitarians, while accepting the need for personal autonomy, are concerned that the focus on the individual can crowd out concern for the welfare of others. Accordingly, they oppose the idea that more advantaged individuals should be able to exercise personal choices which undermine social cohesion or limit the opportunities for others, such as a decision by affluent parents to send their children to schools outside their immediate vicinity, which undermines the long-term viability of the local school relied upon by less prosperous parents. From this more communitarian perspective, social policies should be designed in ways that encourage individuals to be concerned for the well-being of their neighbours as much as themselves.

CENTRALISM OR LOCALISM

One of the continuing dilemmas facing Labour is the tension between central forms of planning and control which aim to equalize life chances and service availability and the autonomy of localities. Should central direction take precedence over local decision making in order to ensure that all citizens, regardless of location, are provided with equally good access to high-quality educational, health and social care services? Or should localities be able to develop more 'bespoke' services or support networks in response to 'popular' demands from within their local community? To what extent should wealthier communities be expected to share their resources with less prosperous ones?

Although there has always been a lively debate on the Left as to whether the local or central state in a capitalist society is capable of furthering the interests of the disadvantaged as opposed to the powerful, there has been a noticeable loss of confidence amongst the reformist Left about the positive potential of state action at either level. One of the reasons, for example, that 'Blue' Labour has attracted so much attention is because its criticisms of top-down 'mechanical' forms of statism seemed to resonate across the Left. From a Blue Labour perspective, it is vital to empower communities and neighbourhoods and to encourage greater dialogue, deliberation and participation at the local level. During this process, communities would begin to determine their own priorities and solutions to the problems they wish to resolve. Inevitably, this process will give rise to significant differences in terms of the range and quality of local services. Such postcode differences are welcomed by Blue Labour as it is seen as an essential aspect of revitalizing public engagement with the political process.

While there is considerable merit in community activity of this kind, 'state' socialists are rightly concerned that citizens' hard-won welfare 'rights' may be put at risk in the process. Clearly, it is one thing to have active communities pressing for enhanced forms of security and opportunity but quite another if they are pressing to reduce entitlements or services that have a disproportionate impact on less popular groups within the locality. Moreover, although there might be issues where it is possible to generate a loose-knit 'progressive' consensus, such as campaigning for a living wage, it is likely to prove much harder to secure agreement about the allocation of a scarce resource such as social housing, in which the more pressing needs of new arrivals in the area have to be balanced against those who have been waiting patiently in line. Subsidiarity and double devolution are attractive theoretical constructs but they may give rise to 'non-socialist' outcomes. Although it is true that most welfare services are delivered at the local level, the key question is whether these should be of a predictable, standardized kind thereby mirroring the quality of a standard meal on the menu of a popular nationwide restaurant chain or of a more unpredictable kind (a one-off local establishment) which holds out the prospect of an exceptional experience but, equally, a more forgettable one. For egalitarian centralists, the ultimate goal is to deliver a standardized, nationwide range of high-quality services with minimal local variation save for demographic considerations which might determine the precise mix of provision. In contrast, those who stress the importance of localism are so concerned about central insensitivity to local needs and preferences that they are willing to trade off equality for autonomy. This leads on to the issue of universalism and diversity.

UNIVERSALISM OR DIVERSITY

Universalism has come to be regarded as a key, if not exclusive, feature of a socialist welfare state. It recognizes that citizens have similar needs for income security, education and health care and that these are best met through collective measures designed to ensure that no individual has to bear the inordinate costs associated with long-term illness, disability or unemployment. Universal provision is also seen as having a key role in breaking down socially constructed divisions based on class, gender and ethnicity thereby enhancing social solidarity. This inclusive dimension of universalism has not always operated effectively in practice. Indeed, critics have argued that the elasticity of the concept has served to mask highly differentiated forms of eligibility resulting in some citizens being denied services or being offered inferior services. It has also been argued that universalism is much more likely to take root in socially homogeneous societies, and in eras when class antagonisms have softened, such as the aftermath of the Second World War. Accordingly, universalism is deemed to be less suited to societies with greater cultural diversity and where individuals and groups accord greater importance to differences rather than to similarities. Indeed, it can be argued that such inequities can be exacerbated as a result of the 'difference-blind rules and institutions' associated with universalism.[6] The question that arises is whether universalism can be adapted to encompass this growing emphasis on diversity. Clearly, cash benefits permit recipients to exercise choice in terms of expenditure. In the case of services, though, this is much more problematic. Should socialists encourage an ever-wider range of specialist provision and individual payments to accommodate differences based on gender, sexuality or culture or should the aim be to ensure that universal services are modified and developed to reflect degrees of difference?

PUBLIC OR NON-PUBLIC WELFARE PROVISION

Since the establishment of the postwar welfare state, questions have been raised about whether it can be assumed that publicly provided welfare services will necessarily be qualitatively superior to private or voluntary provision because of the absence of the profit motive and the selfless ethos and professional expertise of staff. Both Blue and Purple Labour have expressed scepticism about 'traditionalist' socialist arguments of this kind, believing that the unitarist standpoint needs to be subjected to rigorous appraisal and change not least because of growing demographic and financial pressures. These 'new' revisionists believe that there should be an increase in personalized provision and budgets, greater user choice, competition and enhanced forms of co-production. Accordingly, greater reliance on co-operatives, mutual and social enterprises is seen as the way forward.

While there would be much to gain from an expansion of such activity in relation to private sector activity, it is questionable whether the public sector will be improved by developments of this kind. A well-performing public agency should always ensure, and expect, that both those providing the service and those using it are able to feed back their opinions and be actively involved in reshaping provision in the light of technological developments and changing preferences. 'Voice' of this kind has always been a vital component of socialist social policy.[7] However, the embrace of neo-liberal-inspired public management systems has weakened the power of voice in many organizations with the result that cost-cutting changes have been introduced which have demoralized staff and users alike. The remedy is to ensure that more collaborative forms of working and provision are restored rather than encouraging a plethora of new providers who will be unable to guarantee the continuity of high-quality services. Moreover, while personal 'welfare' budgets have proved popular with some groups of users, enabling them to by-pass 'inflexible' state provision, this is unlikely to ensure that the root causes of service deficiencies, such as an inadequate supply of well-trained care staff, is resolved. A publicly funded, integrated state health and social care service is much more likely, for example, to ensure that all citizens, regardless of class, gender, race or locality are provided with the 'personalized' forms of high-quality support they need.

Labour now needs to adopt the bolder approach to social policy pursued by the Attlee governments in the face of the much harsher economic circumstances that existed in the late 1940s and early 1950s. This will require a clearer vision of what constitutes the next stage in Labour's transformation of society. This will include measures to ensure a more egalitarian distribution of income and wealth, guarantees of high-quality welfare services for all across the life cycle and a willingness to campaign vigorously for the positive advantages that a more equal and solidaristic society will bring. It will involve challenging the vested interests of those with excessive wealth and power who continue to promote the idea that the highly inequitable economic and social arrangements that currently prevail in British society and beyond are natural, merited and functional. After all, as Harold Wilson once famously said, the Labour Party has little or no purpose if it abandons its transformative 'moral' crusade.

NOTES

1. J. Nuttall, *Psychological Socialism*, Manchester: Manchester University Press, 2004; p.192
2. F. Field, *The State of Dependency*, London: Social Market Foundation, 2000
3. A. Park, E. Clery, J. Curtice, M. Phillips and D. Utting (eds.) *British Social Attitudes 28*, Sage: London, 2012
4. J. Le Grand, *The Other Invisible Hand*, Princeton: Princeton University Press, 2007
5. H. Berggren and L. Tragardh, 'Pippi Longstocking: The Autonomous Child and the Moral Logic of the Swedish Welfare State' in H. Mattsson and S-O. Wallenstein (eds.) *Swedish Modernism: Architecture, Consumption and the Welfare State*, London: Black Dog, 2010; pp.50–65
6. A. Anttonen, L. Haikio and K. Stefansson (eds.), *Welfare State, Universalism and Diversity*, Cheltenham: Edward Elgar, 2012
7. A.O. Hirschman, *Exit, Voice, and Loyalty* (new edition), Cambridge, Mas.: Harvard University Press, 1990

Part III

A SOCIAL DEMOCRATIC STATE

Chapter 11

IN PRAISE OF CENTRALISM

David Walker

Bowing to pressure from the Royal British Legion, the Cameron government executed a swerving U-turn and has reverted to a Labour-era proposal to create a chief coroner. Coroners, it was contended, could not cope with the growing complexity of death, for example among soldiers and aircrew serving in Afghanistan. On behalf of relatives (and the Armed Forces) the Legion said coroners' investigations had to be more orderly and predictable. The only way forward was supervision and quality control through a new central office. The senior lawyer appointed to it promised to remedy 'lack of consistency, lack of leadership and lack of guidance'.

Inquest juries and coroners' courts had been *inconsistent*. Critics of 'centralism' don't always grasp the social, political and also the cultural importance of standardization, regularity and evenness in public affairs, and the enduring effectiveness of strong central government in delivering them.

It's true that modernism has travelled in opposing directions. In culture and the arts, unpredictability and inconsistency are favoured as cousins of originality – neophilia rules OK. Modern (indeed postmodern) sensibility prizes diversity. The individualism now prevalent in our society often strives to buck uniformity and consistency. 'Post-Ford', economic progress is supposed to depend on innovativeness, atypicality, absence of routine.

But the individualism that marks culture and economy also insists on *equal treatment* and exceptionless respect for the individual, and jibs at random outcomes. What the Royal British Legion and the chief coroner found unacceptable in the operation of inquests was the prospect of dissimilar outcomes in court proceedings where circumstances and expectations were similar. Equality before the law and in public services implies they will be administered evenly, according to predetermined standards. Similarity, predictability, even uniformity: these are the stock in trade of central administration.

Central government is best placed to guarantee fair and equal treatment and individual rights. Is it a paradox that the embodiment of the nation's collective purposes (the state) underpins individual rights? No, Professor John Dunn observed. Historically, 'the idea of the modern state and the idea of human rights are very elaborately interrelated with one another'; egalitarianism has pushed the growth of central government.

As modern sensibility absorbed strong ideas of fairness (and has held on to them, despite the parliamentary triumph of the Tories) so people have become less tolerant of differentiation – of life chances, in public services, or of consequences of any given behaviour. They become more insistent that government eradicate perceived inequalities, a demand that looks likely to survive Cameron's state-shrinking administration.

In this chapter my task is to pit the continuing, willed necessity of strong central government against critics, including on the Left the mutualists and localists, arguing for less central power, more space for voluntary and community activity. Against them 'necessity' may ring as too strong a word, but a brief reading of the historical record supports it. Voluntarism and localism have been tried and failed. They decayed for very good reasons. Mutualism was found wanting in the face of private economic power and capitalism's protean strength.

Victorian Big Society was dominated by aristocrats and tight-fisted employers. They could not or would not remedy the defects of industrial capitalism and, for the sake of social order as much as to sustain capitalist accumulation, the central state was remade so that it could intervene – to secure public health, working-class housing and schools. Those interventions ramified once the state was democratized and Labour came to power.

The Fabians (as later in the twentieth century Neville Chamberlain, once a progressive Tory minister of health, and after him the Attlee government) did not trample on voluntary and local flowers: offices and departments of state were sucked into a vacuum. The Labour Party took the parliamentary road because the interests of working people could only be protected through national legislation, for example to mitigate the power of private employers, which no amount of local action could accomplish. Why didn't Clement Attlee, a strong believer in the 'associative principle' remain in the voluntary sector or, having been Mayor of Stepney, stay in local government? He saw that the realization of local objectives – the equalization of resources and their fair distribution – demanded state action, directed from the centre.

When economic capacity was evacuated from places, local government was impotent. Liverpool City Council could not arrest the decline of transatlantic shipping nor Newcastle do much about the combination of boardroom incompetence and union short-termism among Tyneside shipbuilders. Industrial reorganization, whether in its 1930s' form or its present post-crash manifestations, demands the strength and strategic capacity of the centre.

Progressives will always be centralizers because fairness necessitates national formulae, for distributing money, for rationalizing the public business; in regulation, as in public service delivery, there are inescapable and centralizing logics of scale, bound up with the advance of technology and the deepening of professional expertise. Bureaucracy, as Professor Nicholas Deakin has said, is a device for achieving equity by sustaining common standards, providing a framework for support and above all fairness in resource allocation.

If the contours of the state have changed, the dynamism of centralization has not. A contemporary example is equalities. Modern sensibilities simply will not countenance someone who is black or lesbian being treated differently on the whim or will of one organization or in one place. So we hear, as it were, advocates of respect for diversity crying 'all power to the centre' – because only central government is able to decree, across the space in which its jurisdiction runs, that the same equalities agenda applies.

Yet nowadays statism has few friends. Strong central government is assailed from the Left as well as, more predictably, from the Right. The Fabian tradition has been recast as a history of oppression, the Webbs outed as authoritarians. Poor Douglas Jay's posterity is that remark about the man in Whitehall knowing best. Mutualism, localism, the recovery of Labour's voluntaristic roots – here is where the think tank action is, where the kids whizz.

Of course English/UK central government is deficient. The civil service is clapped out. Financial relations between the tiers of (English) government are perverse and wasteful. The centre, like local government, is riven and siloed. And of course (and at all levels

of governance) public mistrust, indifference and ignorance are unde-
niable. But all that gives urgency to restating the principled case for
centralism – shorthand for a strong, resourceful government at the
hub of the polity.

The case revolves around redistributive capacity. It's about the
power to concentrate the supply of scarce resources, human and
financial, in order to spread them more fairly. Taxable capacity is
maximized at the larger scale, and that will tend to be national – a
truth recognized by the Normans, which is why King William I did
not localize fiscal data collection and his Domesday Book was a single
central entity. Paradoxically, centralism gives the political and fiscal
capacity to underpin both individual freedom and human rights and
the capacity of localities to exercise maximum self-determination.

Let's start with the permanent asymmetry of needs and resources.
Inequalities across the territory are marked by the obvious differentiation of places by income, property and other wealth. Spatial inequity
mirrors and focuses inequality of income and wealth between classes
and sectors. The case for a strong centre is cast-iron. Unless it can
collect and redistribute revenue, poor places can only get poorer.

Whatever happens in other countries, residents in England
(and to a large extent in the other parts of the UK) have long been
remarkably intolerant of and successful in resisting locally organized
taxation. Local government was losing civic and service functions
long before Margaret Thatcher came to power. That resulted from
the inability and unwillingness of local property owners (ratepayers)
to support even minimal levels of social provision, forcing the centre
to pay to intervene. In the 1890s Lord Salisbury increased grants to
local authorities not because the Tories were generous but because
local party members demanded 'rate relief'.

Workable localism is posterior to and dependent on much greater
income equality than has been the pattern in England, which is why
stronger local government works in, say, Sweden. Localism might
work if there were unity between need and capacity to pay – if residents and service users all lived in higher band properties or enjoyed
higher incomes. They don't. Borough boundaries are often walls
around financially favoured enclaves; neighbours have needs but no
money. So, where public services are organized on progressive principles – that is to say, not based on ability to pay – we need centralism.

If need and taxable capacity are misaligned, which they are across
the territory of England outside the south-east, providing decent

services to lower income households will depend on a non-local agent (the central state) both to detect need (that may be occluded locally) and to pay to meet it (because the locality cannot afford to). And the centre will often see need that locality refuses to recognize – which was the historical background against which grants and compulsion grew in the last century, for housing, schooling, health and so on.

The existing capacity of HM Revenue & Customs leaves a lot to fret about as it seeks to fight tax evaders and greedy corporates with reduced budgets. But imagine tax-gathering capacity were split and spread. How would a regional tax inspector fare against a multinational corporate? If recalcitrant taxpayers can frighten governments by threatening to move to less exacting jurisdictions abroad, what would householders and businesses say and do if tax rates started to vary significantly between localities? Actually, that is an academic question because business has already secured the nationalization of property taxation, and changes in the regime proposed by the Cameron government will not dent the basic standardization of the small amount of tax levied on business property.

A second argument is about capacity and knowledge. Economic power is exercised directly by the boards of private firms making short-term decisions about the location of capital investment and jobs and indirectly through consultants, credit-rating agencies or participants in hedge funds. Both ways, the public interest depends on countervailing power, to use J.K. Galbraith's old phrase, and for most practical purposes that is going to mean central government – the only entity that can sequester their assets and, in the case of the UK, exercise a degree of monetary and financial control over the markets in which they operate. The exhibition of national sovereignty may have left a lot to be desired in recent times, but the singularity and necessity of strong (nation) states and effective central government within them is clear.

There's a broader point about government's cognitive capacity. Professional excellence is limited across most disciplines. They may include politics and certainly include public management and the technical skills of governance. Scarce skill needs to be concentrated, at the centre. As technology and globalization expand opportunities for criminals, so public protection needs to become more sophisticated, more adept, and that must mean specialization and focus. Certain public goods are 'big', too large for localities and regions to handle – scientific and medical research capacity and world-class universities are examples. To stop their necessary auto-nomy becoming institutional selfishness, strong central frameworks are needed.

Just as clinical expertise in handling stroke and heart failure needs to be marshalled into a limited number of specialist centres, so quality in public services is likely to be maximized thanks to central planning of how to allocate professional knowledge. An arm's-length central body such as the Environment Agency can pull together specialist knowledge about flooding, then make it (and resources) available locally, on the basis of a (centralized) risk assess-ment. Sometimes that 'technocratic' assessment of flood risk may override the vocal demands of a community, for the good reason that the inhabitants of a single place can never see the whole picture. Rationing, which is endemic to public goods, is centralizing. Empi-rical studies of local resilience in the face of disasters and emergencies have underlined the irreplaceable role of central authorities in dis-seminating information, smoothing bargains and negotiating how resources are managed. Insurance systems become more effective the larger the population they cover; risk will tend to be easier to mitigate at scale. Procurement costs can usually be cut, the larger the number of units being bought for. Where but the centre can the future be modelled, personnel numbers calculated and training organized?

Critics of centralism often invoke 'community', meaning people's capacity to self-organize at local level. National formulae, it is argued, ride roughshod over local characteristics and expressions of identity. But a strong counterargument is that community often hides need and excludes people. When community expresses class interest, the central state alone can protect the oppressed. The Tories of Westminster are demonstrating how their presentation of the borough interest penalizes (indeed is seeking to exclude and even expel) poorer households. Rich areas may refuse to raise taxation on the grounds that better-off households don't need services. But the poor households in their midst may have strong needs, which may only be identified thanks to centrally run programmes and mandates. Looked-after children, travellers, the indigent, the men-tally ill: they may be victims of 'community' and can be rescued only by central oversight and central administrative power.

Central government has the biggest backyard. That allows it to be disinterested. Residents in the Chilterns or in Lincolnshire may try to prohibit development or block infrastructure. They are not minded to think of their neighbours' interests, which may be furthered by the development. But central government must. Railways, wind farms, housing: they have to be planned, which will mean adopting a strategic vision at the widest possible level, and tests of relative benefit and utility applied. Localism exacerbates housing shortage because the interests of the possessors in maintaining their backyards take precedence over those of non-residents and aspirant residents. Of course norms of procedural fairness have to be upheld but ultimately the interests of the majority have to prevail.

In a time of fiscal constraint, making service delivery effective and efficient demands ever more sophisticated methods, and more knowledge, especially financial. To maximize value for money we need the fullest flow of performance data, which allows benchmarking and comparison between organizations. The organizations themselves cannot be entirely trusted – they may bend the data and game the system. Only central government can insist on definitions and standards, require data to be collected, and inspect to see that it happens.

Audit and regulation augment knowledge, and they have to be stipulated by central government. Arguing about how much audit and regulation does not detract from the need for some. A flaw in the Cameron government's thinking about open data is the absence of specification. Data about spending and performance come in all shapes and sizes. They need to be standardized, validated, analysed; in short they have to be bureaucratized.

Central government is not going to wither away, however fraught the present day struggle over the size and shape of the state, pushed by the Cameron government's ideological commitment to dismemberment and business takeover of its functions. For one reason, international pressures and security risks are unlikely to abate: neither Ayn Rand conservatives nor Left localists say much about migration, terrorism or, for that matter, continent-spanning banks, Chinese capitalists and foreign fraudsters. That's because only government can put up a shield. When it comes to movement of people, goods and capital, there is nothing else around.

But the telling arguments are domestic. As long as progressives string together sentences about protecting the vulnerable, levelling life chances, securing justice between generations, preventing place becoming destiny, mitigating the power of capital and the expendability (in the eyes of corporate boards) of people and communities, then their subject will remain the central state.

Chapter 12

A DEMOCRATIC SOCIALIST CASE FOR THE UNION

David S. Moon

Only Labour can truly claim to be the party of both the Union and devolution. Despite their full title, the Conservative and Unionist party are a significant electoral force in southern England alone and sport a leadership at Westminster only recently reconciled to devolution. Neither Plaid Cymru nor the Scottish National Party desire devolution: their ultimate desire being to break up the Union. The Liberal Democrats and their antecedents have been the longest and most consistent supporters of devolution within the Union; however, their minority status has ceded them a secondary role historically, reliant on another to institute their constitutional dreams. It was a Labour government which brought about devolution to Scotland, Wales and Northern Ireland[1] and only Labour, of the two parties with the potential to form a majority government at Westminster, commands significant support across England, Scotland and Wales. Unlike its fellow British-wide parties, Labour is Unionist for reasons of political philosophy *and* electoral need.

Out of power today with the exception of the Welsh Assembly government – where a working majority is lacked – Labour is besieged with advice as to how it should move forward. This includes the party embracing nationalist language and sentiments of one form or another. Labour, it is declared, needs to be more 'Welsh' in Wales and more 'Scottish' in Scotland (and while we're at it, more 'English' in

England); or, conversely, to grasp the uniting power of 'Britishness' as a collective identity. Yet the first route has already been tried to increasing degrees, especially in Wales, with concerning effect, while when the latter route has been articulated it has shown itself an unpalatable prospect – 'British jobs for British workers' anyone?

If Labour is to be a 'One Nation' party, this is not what the phrase must mean. Embracing nationalism to fight nationalism, *in whatever form*, is the wrong route for Labour to take; rather its identity as a Unionist *and* devolutionist party should be proudly affirmed as part of an emphasis upon universal socialist values which override geographical and cultural boundaries. Practically and rhetorically, this means advancing an *inter*nationalist social democratic politics of which Unionism, at its best, is a key part.

This is not an argument about the correct degree of constitutional devolution Labour should seek. It is about how the party articulates its politics and policies. This approach, founded upon a more direct, less evasive differentiation between Labour's constitutive parts, necessitates greater intellectual and political bravery. In the long term, however, it would ultimately benefit the party, its values and the people it is meant to represent, as well as harden the Union.

REJECTING NATIONALISM

The argument for – and adoption of – a shift in Labour's language to an emphasis upon national specificity, especially in Wales, is partly explained by the rise of nationalist tendencies within the party which long pre-existed devolution, and partly as an attempt to spike the nationalists' guns (Labour suffered an existential crisis at the 2007 elections when both Plaid and the SNP were elevated from parties of opposition to ones of government).

Another key reason is surely pragmatic – and points to a key issue yet to be solved by socialists in Britain: how to deal with intra-party ideological differentiation. The UK has a multi-level system of governance and Labour has inevitably made a muddled shift from a solidly Unitary party into a non-formally multi-level party, with interlinked but distinct identities and structures at devolved, central and supranational EU levels. Just as the UK is a Union of 'nations within a nation', within the post-devolution multi-level context Labour appears increasingly to be an institution of parties within a party.

Conventional wisdom stated that Tony Blair's brand of 'New' Labour was never going to be as popular in Scotland or Wales as across Britain's key marginal seats. Different electoral calculations and freedom from the centrist-drag of 'middle England' voters thus means a more evidently social democratic politics was both possible and necessary in the devolved polities. The devolved Labour administrations (and attendant Scottish and Welsh Labour parties) therefore felt the need to differentiate themselves from the 'Blairite' Westminster government, working to forge separate identities for themselves, distinct from that of the Labour government at Westminster – key to this was the pursuance of policy differentiation.

However, recognizing that the media and opposition would leap upon any sign of 'split and division' between the party's devolved and central levels, means were required to justify and trumpet policy differences whilst avoiding criticizing the Blair/Brown leadership. This causes a structural problem for Labour whereby the leaders in Holyrood and Cardiff Bay feel it necessary to defer to London on issues which are not devolved matters, refusing to express an opinion where it might be contentious. A squirm-inducing non-answer from Rhodri Morgan during a 2006 BBC *Question Time* demonstrated this problem perfectly. Asked for his views on the Iraq war, Morgan told the unimpressed audience:

I don't know because I have not looked at the issues because I'm not in the House of Commons – I left it to the MPs in the House of Commons. There are 660 of them doing that job. If I had been in the House of Commons, not only would [people] have heard my views, they would have actually seen which way my hand went up. That's the key thing – that's their job, it's not my job.[2]

Labour ministers in Scotland and Wales thus naturally sought a depoliticized language to explain-away policy divergence and muffle ideological disagreements. Sadly such depoliticization has often meant embracing justifications for differences based upon their necessity due to reasons of national specificity. Hence, in Wales, Labour resorts to talk of 'made in Wales' policies which draw upon a specific 'small-nation psychology' meeting particular 'Welsh needs'. It does not feel strained, however, to reason that Morgan's administration rejected the private finance initiative (PFI) in NHS Wales, for example, not because – as he claimed – 'greater consumer choice in public services does not fit in with *Welsh values*',[3] but because his administration judged it a neo-liberal, right-wing policy which went against Labour's social democratic principles.

Such rhetoric was easy, emotive and effective, but the wrong means to demonstrate independence of mind. As Trench argues, '[i]n a Scottish or Welsh arena, when the issues can be defined primarily in Scottish or Welsh terms, the debate is framed in terms that structurally advantage the nationalist parties'.[4] Relying upon political rhetoric which emphasizes national specificity thus weakens the position of both unionist parties and, relatedly, the Union as a whole. Indeed, if the choice is between two varieties of social democratic politics, each claiming to be explicitly tailored to nation-specific needs or 'cultures', electors may well judge one surplus to requirements.

In the 2012 Scottish devolved election Alex Salmond did the seemingly impossible by forming a majority SNP administration – defying an electoral system constructed to prevent such an eventuality – subsequently initiating a forthcoming referendum on Scottish independence. With Salmond, Scotland has a leader perfectly willing to be vocal where he sees the Westminster government – be it Labour or Conservative – is going wrong, demonstrating an independence of mind the Labour administrations arguably lacked. Labour is disproportionately reliant on Scotland and Wales for MPs (hence being Unionist by electoral need) and devolution was meant to protect Labour's 'Celtic' seats. Is Scottish Labour so sure that, if they play politics on nationalist ground that they, not the majority-winning SNP, will triumph? More than electorally, however, such approaches are wrong in so far as they strengthen nationalism against international politics.

Introducing his novel *Mother Night*, Kurt Vonnegut warns: 'Be careful what you pretend to be because you are what you pretend to be.' With this in mind the question is therefore posed: while true that the nationalists fell back to third place in Wales at the 2012 elections, if such set-backs are in part due to Labour's 'Welsh-ified' rhetoric, is this a genuinely positive outcome? Or does it rather provide succour for what former Plaid MP Adam Price described as his party's Gramscian 'war of position' with its long-term aim of co-opting the hegemonic force, pulling Labour in a nationalist direction?[5] As Leanne Wood, leader of Plaid, told the *Guardian* when questioned on her party's relative lack of success compared to the SNP in Scotland:

> If you are talking about the success of the national parties, you've got a point. But the Welsh nationalist agenda has progressed quite significantly since the setting up of devolution. What we've seen happening in Wales is that the British parties, the unionist parties, have taken on a lot of the policies that we've been advocating.[6]

If national distinctiveness becomes a central prop of Labour's rhetoric and policy style it will articulate a nationalist politics; if Labour articulates a nationalist politics then it becomes, in effect, a nationalist party; and if the two major parties in the devolved polities are ultimately nationalist, the politics of Wales and Scotland will be lost to nationalism, whether separatist or culturist. Beyond betraying the party's ideological internationalism (see below) and framing politics on the nationalist parties' terms, this route also brings dangers for Labour itself, internally.

Founding policy choices upon national differences allowed the devolved Labour parties greater governmental autonomy, but arguably weakened their influence within the wider party. Much has been made of the devolved legislatures' roles as 'laboratories' for developing policy ideas and Carwyn Jones, as the highest elected Labour figure in Britain post-2010, proclaims his administration's ability to '[set] out an alternative vision to people right across the UK'.[7] However, actual uptake of ideas implemented in Wales and Scotland has been minimal by the central party and this may, again, be a further result of a focus on 'nation-specific' policies: policies created to meet Country A's particular needs/values are, logically, not designed to fit Country B. The devolved party levels should aim to build bridges across Britain's borders rather than flooding them with 'clear red water', looking and talking outward as well as inward and formulating policy 'compounds' accordingly.

Whilst gaining them autonomy, such self-regarding politics may well, therefore, have weakened the devolved parties' influence within the wider Labour movement. This may not have been so much the case in Scotland where the last Labour Cabinets were filled with Scots – although post-Brown this will change – but it certainly has been in Wales. For a party which once had a propensity for its 'big beasts' holding Welsh seats – Hardie, Bevan, Callaghan, Foot, Kinnock – the general paucity of Welsh MPs in the Blair/Brown cabinets, outside those who held the posts of secretary of state for Wales and Northern Ireland (i.e. Hain and Murphy) was remarkable. Disconnection from the party leadership still appears evident. At the Cardiff hustings in the 2010 Labour leadership contest, the candidates appeared universally oblivious to audible tensions over the raised question of furthering powers to the Assembly, whilst the eventual victor Ed Miliband's inability to name all candidates in the following Scottish Labour leadership contest spoke volumes. Continuing disconnect risks damaging the integrated linkages which bind together the party as a British-wide political force.

So Labour needs to find a new way to debate within itself – a way that it can articulate its politics while maintaining the internal autonomy of its Welsh and Scottish branches, without diluting their influence, or damaging the vertical integration of the post-devolution party's multiple levels. To this end, rejecting the above route, Labour must return to first principles, to its position as the party of both devolution *and* the Union. This is *not* to argue for a less devolved Labour, nor any reversal of the devolved settlement: it in no way indicates that the party/ies in Wales and Scotland should not continue to adopt policies or identities which diverge from those advocated at the central party level – only that those policies and identities be articulated in a particular manner.

REFORMING UNIONISM

Labour is Unionist by political philosophy because it is an *inter-nationalist* party, a fraternal stance which applies as much to the people of the nations within the UK as those outside of it. Gordon Brown sought to strengthen solidaristic links between these peoples by tying them together into a narrative of Britishness which, though much repeated, failed to connect. Under Ed Miliband, Labour's answer seems to be to defend the Union by starting a debate over 'Englishness'; Labour, the claim goes, needs to embrace and articulate an English identity in England, seemingly mirroring the view that the party must articulate 'Welshness' in Wales and 'Scottishness' in Scotland. The answer to nationalism should not, however, be more nationalism, but rather the assertion of its opposite – of internationalism, as embodied in the Union.

In the narrative of the Labour movement, the institutions which unite the peoples of England, Scotland and Wales are not the monarchy, Christianity, and memorializations of the Empire, but rather the National Health Service, Trade Union Congress and British Broadcasting Corporation. None of these – NHS, TUC or BBC – are monolithic, monadic entities; each has its national-regional branches and variants with different structures, campaigns and programming. Yet all of these cross-border institutions belong to the *people* of the United Kingdom, enshrining in their own ways universal concepts such as equality, solidarity and the value of education and culture, which lie at the heart of the Labour tradition. The Unionist impulse is a part of this, being a facet of the socialist belief that what unites us, regardless of nationality, is greater than what divides us – that we are stronger together than apart. Such philosophical universalism is at the heart of trade unionism and the social democratic creed of equality and was summed up nicely by Leo Abse's 1976 declaration – channelling Nye Bevan – that 'a steelworker is a steelworker, whether he works in Ebbw Vale, Llanwern, Scunthorpe or Sheffield and... a fibre worker is a fibre worker, whether he works in Pontypool or Harrogate'.[8] In this regard, the rhetoric of 'One Nation' makes sense.

But here's the rub. Abse's statement was meant as an attack upon retarded nationalism *and* devolution, which he believed would betray the Labour movement's internationalism by institutionalizing nationalist divisions within the working-class of Great Britain. Power, he argued, should therefore remain centrally held at the Westminster Parliament. This argument was made at perhaps its most eloquent by Neil Kinnock, when he told the House in 1975:

> If I had to use a label of any kind, I should have to call myself a 'unionist'. However, I am a unionist entirely for reasons of expediency. I believe that the emancipation of the class that I have come to this House to represent, unapologetically, can best be achieved in a single nation and in a single economic unit, by which I mean a unit where we can have a brotherhood of all nations and have the combined strength of working-class people throughout the whole of the United

Kingdom brought to bear against any bully... [The working class's] misfortunes are not the result of being British,
Welsh or Scottish. They have come about because their fate
has been, in the system of economic organization or disor-
ganization that we have had hitherto, to be workers...[9]

As conceived of by Kinnock and Abse, 'a single nation' and 'a single
economic unit' precluded anything but a unitary state model; the
pluralism of nationalism would therefore undermine the operation
of nationalization as a key tenet of centralized socialist economic
planning.

This goes to the heart of two problems contemporary Unionism
encounters. First, Unionism is equated with an anti-devolutionist
position. Logically, the belief in the Union – that is, in support for
the continued existence of Great Britain as a single state – precedes
any preference for particular constitutional settlements therein.
However, as Conservative AM David Melding notes, 'in practice
Unionism, as an ideology, has rarely disguised its zeal to preserve
a unitary and centralized United Kingdom'.[10] Second, Unionism
is equated not with the rejection of nationalism but assertion of a
British nationalism; Gerry Hassan charges it with being 'the majority
nationalism of these isles' arguing that 'British Labour is, for all its
talk of internationalism, a British nationalist party, and one which
has consistently failed to advocate a counter-story to the Tory account
of "the Conservative nation".'[11] Together, these interpretations mean
the label 'Unionist' has become a lazy term of abuse amongst certain
tendencies inside and outside Labour.

There is much to be said, historically, in support of both views;
however, the modern social democratic Unionism which Labour
needs today should resolutely mean neither interpretation. Unionism
is not antithetical with support for devolution and the label Unionist
should not be axiomatically equated with an anti-devolution
stance. Unionism needn't simply mean centralism – though its
reclaiming would hopefully allow mature debates over this, shorn
of the nationalist rhetoric of what different nations 'deserve'.
Simultaneously, support for devolution need not mean a lack of
support for the Union; the two positions should not be mutually
exclusive. Nor should Unionism be viewed as British nationalism any
more than a devolutionist be immediately tarred a Welsh/Scottish

nationalist. The label must be reclaimed by social democrats: Unionism refers to a belief simply in an inter-national *union* of peoples – 'the brotherhood of all nations', in Kinnock's words – or 'One Nation' in Ed Miliband's. It is from here that Labour must return and start anew.

REAFFIRMING A 'ONE NATION' UNIONISM

Here is the route forward: the Labour Party, across Britain, needs to reject the evasive, naturalizing language of the-nation-as-justification (whether with reference to apparent Welsh, Scottish, English or British requisites) and repoliticize its internal differences, where they exist. The Unionist label in Wales and Scotland has become shorthand for lick-spittle supporters of the party leadership's political approach – *it should be exactly the opposite.* It should be the Unionists position to call for socialism, leaving the nationalists to fawn and excuse as they explain away their own 'rebellious' policies on conservative, nationalist grounds. This route would require bravery; the language of national necessity has hugely effective rhetorical appeal, whereas justifications on the basis of equality, class and solidarity seem 'harder sells', even before factoring in the danger of attacks upon a 'split' party. But such is having the courage of one's convictions.

Labour is 'the People's Party' and must relearn to speak for the *people* of Britain – the *people* of England, Wales and Scotland and not the *British* people, or the disaggregated *Welsh* and *Scottish* people, and so forth. If Labour speaks for 'One Nation' *this* is what it must mean: the union of people, amassed. Reaffirming such a social democratic Unionism provides solid foundations for Labour philosophically and electorally and charts the best route forward to grapple with the present state of the Union: a Britain increasingly divided by geography and class, which fails working people and mistreats the most vulnerable in favour of the most secure.

NOTES

1. Regarding the Union, the chapter focuses only upon Scotland, Wales and England where Labour organizes electorally. Northern Ireland is another case in itself

2. BBC News 'Morgan refuses to give Iraq views', *BBC News Online*. 3 February 2006: http://news.bbc.co.uk/1/hi/wales/4675922.stm

3. For further examples see: D.S. Moon, 'Rhetoric and Policy Learning: On Rhodri Morgan's "Clear Red Water" and "Made in Wales" Health Policies', *Public Policy and Administration* (2012) published online at: http://ppa.sagepub.com/content/early/2012/08/22/0952076712455821. abstract?rss=1

4. A. Trench, 'Introduction' in A. Trench (ed.) *The State of the Nations 2008*, Exeter: Imprint, 2008; p.16

5. See B. Powys, 'The handshake', *BBC News Online,* 27 June 2007: www. bbc.co.uk/blogs/thereporters/betsanpowys/2007/06/the_handshake. html

6. Quoted in A. Sparrow, 'Plaid Cymru leader: we can only prosper if we do things for ourselves', *Guardian,* 12 September 2012: www.guardian. co.uk/politics/2012/sep/12/plaid-cymru-leader-wales-prosper

7. BBC News 'Welsh Labour shows alternative says Jones', *BBC News Online,* 26 September 2011: www.bbc.co.uk/news/uk-wales-15069391

8. Hansard, HC Deb 16 December 1976, vol. 922, 1793

9. Hansard, HC Deb 3 February 1975, vol. 885, 1031

10. D. Melding, *Will Britain Survive Beyond 2020,* Cardiff: Institute of Welsh Affairs, 2009; p.187

11. D. Alexander and G. Hassan, 'Scotland, nationalism and the left', *Soundings,* 51 (2012), p.20

Chapter 13

LOCAL GOVERNMENT

Simon Slater

The purpose of this chapter is to consider a social democratic model for local government. It will assess how local government can be rejuvenated to promote greater participation and how it can be utilized to achieve civic socialism.

The main thrust will be to argue that greater power should be devolved from central government to local government and in so doing local government will be seen to have a greater influence upon people's lives in terms of the services they use. Devolving power back to local government will help to foster greater civic participation as people realize that local government and local politicians can make a real difference within the communities in which they live, rather than being seen as powerless administrators of central government policy.

The two key areas which this chapter will consider are local government finance and local government service delivery. It will also argue that changing the political structure of local government is not necessarily required and the first steps to rejuvenating local government must be to devolve power within the existing structure.

THE LIMITS OF LOCAL GOVERNMENT

Whilst it is clearly the case that local government requires greater power to be effective, it is important to recognize its limitations. One of the key arguments of the Blairites and their successors is that because of economic globalization all governments must resist the urge to raise marginal rates of tax on the wealthy because doing so will lead to a flight of capital as the wealthy and large multinationals relocate to countries with lower rates of taxation. Thus, as the argument goes, social democrats can no longer tax the wealthy or multinationals too much because doing so would be counterproductive.

Much of the response to this now generally accepted thesis has been to retreat into an agenda of localism to compensate for the perceived limitations of the central state to achieve traditional socialist objectives. However, a retreat into localism is clearly the wrong response to the increased power of multinationals and international financial markets. Local groups such as residents associations clearly cannot and do not have the power to regulate the banking sector or stop the excesses of multinationals. In this sense, whilst giving back greater power to local government is desirable, it is definitely not a response to the important questions of how we can regulate the banking sector and financial markets effectively in a globalized economic climate. Or, how economic growth and globalization can be utilized to benefit everyone in society and not just those at the top, which has been increasingly the case over the past decade.

Some of the recent Labour Party thinking as outlined in *The Purple Book* by the Blairites, and by Blue Labour seems to emphasize localism and is sceptical of the central state. This view appears to be somewhat misguided in terms of answering key questions of regulation and taxation. Indeed, it could be argued that a much stronger central state is required, and, moreover, a government which is more fully prepared to work with other countries to agree joint regulation and even harmonized tax and regulatory structures to combat the power of high finance and multinationals who, at times, appear to work in a moral vacuum. Such joint co-operation between nation states would limit the power of multinationals to play countries off each other for favourable labour and regulatory conditions. These are issues which cannot be answered by a complete retreat into localism. To some degree much of Labour's philosophical retreat into localism as a replacement for the central state can be seen as an overreaction to the Tory's Big Society.

Local government cannot be the only vehicle through which greater economic equality can be achieved. In fact in some areas too much localism would actually work against achieving greater equality. For example, if we wish to achieve greater equality in terms of health and educational outcomes the central state must provide guidelines, targets and finance to support such an agenda. If local government was set completely free it would only massively increase overall inequality as the wealthy shire counties benefited at the expense of the inner cities. In this sense it is crucial that socialists do not see localism and devolution as a replacement for the central state, as only central government can fully promote, and hopefully achieve, greater equality from region to region. Thus the power of the central state to achieve greater equality must be combined with a stronger and greater role for local government.

Therefore, whilst there clearly needs to be an expanded role for local government, devolving power to local councils cannot be seen as the socialist response to all the challenges we face. Indeed, completely retreating into this sphere – as seems to be implied by some – is completely the wrong response especially in terms of combating the casino-style behaviour of our major banks and financial institutions, which cannot be tackled at a local level. Moreover, it is probably the case that even the nation state is not strong enough to tackle such issues and much greater co-operation between countries is needed to stop their excesses. This being said, there is much that local government can do to improve people's lives and promote and implement a social democratic agenda in local communities.

THE ROLE OF LOCAL GOVERNMENT

Much of *The Purple Book*'s contribution to ensuring a greater role for local government was the idea of elected mayors. This was particularly the case in the contributions from Stephen Twigg MP and Lord Adonis. It is my view that introducing directly elected mayors into our major cities will do very little to improve local government, indeed it may have the result of making politicians seem more remote. Furthermore, given the almost completely unenthusiastic response of the electorate to the idea in May 2012 it would seem the entire concept will be off the table for at least the next decade.

One of the major problems facing local government is the complete lack of trust shown to councils from central government. Central government has imposed target after target and has attempted to completely control local government through tying finance to central government objectives. This culture of control and mistrust from central government has given the impression, and often the correct impression, that the role of local government is merely to administer government programmes and initiatives, leaving very limited policy scope for the councils themselves. In a sense, central government has not trusted the outcome of local council elections and has as a consequence sought to control local government activity. Therefore, central government should allow local authorities the democratic freedom to make their own decisions over more issues. By giving councils greater freedom over the services they provide the public would see that local government was not just an administrative body, but one with real power over policy. This would mean political parties who control councils would be elected or kicked out of office based on the quality, scope and value for money of the services they provide, whereas presently local government elections are often seen as being meaningless, or merely a poll through which national parties can assess their own popularity.

Therefore, the current ideas of how to rejuvenate local government seem to focus too heavily on structural changes rather than focusing on devolving power down within the existing structure. It is the contention here that the structure of local government is not necessarily the problem or reason for voter disengagement, but the fact that local councils have become increasingly impotent due to centralizing governments. Indeed, the elections for police and crime commissioners further highlighted the complete lack of enthusiasm the general public have for such structural reforms, given the miserly turnout.

LOCAL GOVERNMENT FINANCE

The main area which would help to rejuvenate local democracy would be giving councils more power on how they raise and spend money.

It must first be said that local government finance cannot and should not be completely set free. This is because there needs to be a redistributional element in local government finance where the wealthiest local authorities help to subsidize the income of the poorer city and urban authorities. This has traditionally been done by the rates levied on business and such a policy should continue, as allowing councils to keep all their business rates would lead to a huge increase in regional inequality.

In terms of finance, local government has very limited control over raising money. The only tool currently available for raising local taxation is through the council tax. However, even here local authorities have been increasingly dictated to in regards to how much they can raise. This is highlighted by the 5% cap increase put on local authorities under the last Labour government. This cynicism has continued under the Tory-led Coalition who have tied council tax increases above 2% for 2013 to a local referendum, which would be very costly to hold. Such policies, by both parties when in government, show a complete lack of faith in local politicians and the democratic outcomes of local elections.

Further, one of the main problems with the council tax system is that it has no automatic increase built into it. Unlike income tax, where the revenues received will increase as economic growth increases, without the need to raise the percentage amount people pay, the value of council tax income actually decreases in real terms every year if it is never increased by local authorities. As it has no automatic escalation built into it, because it is a flat tax rather than a percentage-based tax, local authorities are annually faced with the unpopular and difficult decision of having to raise council tax. This had led to authorities failing to increase council tax by enough to cope with the ever-increasing demands of providing local services.

Therefore, in order for local authorities to raise enough taxable income they need to be set free from central government control. First, a way needs to be found to ensure that the bulk of taxation received by local authorities has an automatic increase built in as the economy grows, just as income tax. This could be done under the present system of council tax. For example, council tax bands could be re-evaluated. Once this was done council tax banding could be levied as a percentage of the mean property value within a given band. However, the key reform would be to allow council tax to increase yearly in direct correlation to certain indices. For example, council tax could automatically increase in line with the rate of inflation, or the average rise in salaries within each region. Finally, councils could increase the council tax above the automatic increase, but such an increase would be subject to a vote of the Full Council. Indeed, councils could even choose to lower the increase or reduce council tax below the automatic increase.

Linked to this, local authorities should be given the freedom to implement some reforms to the council tax system. They should be given the option of introducing a property tax on top of council tax on homes worth over £1 million. This would give local authorities the option of asking the super rich to pay slightly more money to the local council. Such a policy should be appealing to Labour authorities as such a tax could be used for schemes which would benefit the worst off in the community.

Furthermore, as it is likely such reforms would lead to a boost in council funding, local authorities could expand the parameters through which people could receive council tax discounts. Whilst it would still be the case that central government would protect vulnerable groups from council tax anyway, local government could extend the groups or the amount of discount people receive. This would allow Labour authorities to increasingly help those groups of people such as the elderly and hard-working families on low pay. Thus councils could have more discretion in regards to the amount of council tax people pay.

A further reform in terms of finance would be to allow local authorities, if needed, to levy one-off taxes, which could be included with the council tax bill to fund important local infrastructure projects. For example, if a town or city required a new leisure centre or library, the local council should be allowed to levy a one-off tax to help fund the project. This would give local authorities the option of being able to build local infrastructure projects without the need to resort to PFI-style projects, which over the long term have proven extremely costly and have often taken away control of local services from local people and given it to businesses who do not always operate in the public interest.

In sum, local authorities should be given more options in how they raise money and the council tax should be reformed to ensure it generally increases every year as income tax does. Central government should be prepared to trust the local electors. If a particular council raises local taxes too high, or another council cuts services to the bone, it is local electors who have the democratic choice on whether to elect them for another term. Giving councils more freedom in how they raise and spend tax would create more democratic accountability and in the medium-to-long run increase turnout and interest in local government because local people would see that their local politicians actually do have power to increase or cut spending on key services they use.

FREEDOM OVER SERVICE PROVISION

One of the major problems with the current local government set-up is that local authorities lack autonomy in too many areas. This is highlighted in how local services are provided and set up. An important reform would be to allow local councils the freedom to decide how their own services are provided, whether it is waste collection, road maintenance or leisure services. Councils should not be forced by central government to contract out services to private companies. Local authorities should be given the choice as to how they provide their own services. For example, if a council decides that waste collection would provide a better service if it was done in-house, the authority should be allowed to make this choice. Similarly, if they decide that a certain service would provide the best value for money if it was contracted out, it should be allowed to do so. The key point being that councils should be able to decide themselves how they provide services to the public. If local residents dislike how services are being run, they can change their political leaders at the next local election.

Overall there should be an end to the current assumption and fashion that service delivery is done best by the private sector. In reality this claim seems dubious as there are many services which may well serve the public interest better if they were publicly controlled and thus more accountable for the services they provide to the electorate. As elected councillors would have a greater say in how such previously contracted-out services were run, whether it is leisure centres or waste collection, those services would end up serving local needs better as councillors would react to the wishes of their local electorates. In contrast, services contracted out and run by private companies can often seem aloof and remote from the local electorate with no clear line of accountability and too much focus on profit.

A further area where central government has been dictatorial is in the area of social housing provision. Councils should be given more freedom in how social housing is provided and, importantly, how to increase their housing stocks.

First, central government should not take any of the money raised by local authorities from council house sales. The current Coalition policy of selling council houses at 50% of their value then only giving councils 50% of the total sale does not allow local authorities to replace their lost stock of housing. Indeed, it has the opposite effect of increasing the already overburdened social housing demand. Therefore, local authorities should keep all of the money raised from council house sales and the discount price at which tenants can purchase their council homes should be dramatically reduced, although not scrapped. If councils could keep all the money from the sale of council houses they would have enough money to replace the lost stock and even, over time, increase their stock of social housing.

Second, councils should be allowed to borrow money for investment projects that will pay for themselves over time. Again, the best example here is in the field of social housing. Local authorities should be free to borrow money to invest in their housing stock. This should not just be for small-scale social housing projects, but could be used to increase massively the social housing stock across the country. Such a scheme would allow councils to solve the social housing crisis within a scheme which would be affordable over the long run due to the received rental income. Indeed, for large projects local authorities could work together to increase the social housing stock and this would also help to share the debt burden.

The thrust of this brief analysis has been to outline just a few key areas where reform in local government would have a positive impact upon local communities and devolve power back to local councils. There are also other areas which need to be reformed to allow local councils to be more effective, such as allowing councils to properly hold to account local health and education services which are increasingly aloof from local government scrutiny and accountability, highlighted dramatically with Free Schools and Academies that are not democratically accountable and Health Trusts that can ignore the wishes and the voice of local councils and residents.

Another area of reform is the idea of devolving more decision-making power down to local communities. This would allow local residents, in conjunction with local councillors, to decide how certain pots of money were spent and used in their communities, thus taking away power from the centre of local government.

However, even on this point there are some problems which could lead to greater inequality. Devolving power and budgets down at a local level may well end up benefiting middle-class areas more than deprived inner-city areas as it is the middle class who have the education and skills to exploit such reform. For example, it may be the case that a local group from a middle-class suburb can mitigate the cuts to a library service by volunteering to keep the library open. In the more deprived areas such volunteerism is less likely to happen and as a consequence the library service would merely be cut at the expense of the local community.

Therefore, devolving more power downwards and increasing local volunteerism must not be done as a replacement for services which should be provided by the local authorities. Further, every effort should be made to ensure such devolving of decisions does not disproportionately benefit wealthier areas at the expense of the more deprived ones as this would lead to even more social exclusion and inequality.

Whilst reforms in such areas are necessary, there has not been the relevant space to discuss them in detail here, but it is important to briefly mention the salience of such reforms.

CONCLUSION

The idea of devolving more powers in terms of local government finance and overall service delivery must be seen as only first steps in reforming local government. The important point here is that such reforms would start the gradual process of giving powers back to local councils after decades of increased Whitehall control.

Too much of the debate and ideas surrounding change to local government has merely focused upon changing the structure of how local government is organized. For example, the lack of enthusiasm seen towards the idea of having elected mayors outside of London clearly highlights that overall the general public do not see changing the political structure of local authorities as having any real relevance. Indeed, to many it is merely seen as a costly distraction and a way to increase the amount of politicians at a time when faith in politics is at an all time low. Moreover, as local politicians have very little say and often merely administer central government policy, changing the political structure of local authorities will do very little in terms of devolving actual decision-making power.

Thus this chapter has attempted to focus on key areas where devolving power back to councils within the existing structure, may, over time, allow councils to have a real say over the areas they represent. Making councils more independent in these areas would show that central government trusts local politicians, but more importantly that it trusts local electors to elect people who can actually make decisions that can impact upon their lives. If local councils make poor and unpopular decisions they can be voted out by the electorate, hence real accountability to local government would come from the local electorate and not from endless central government targets. Consequently, the first steps in restoring faith in local government must be a dramatic devolution of powers and responsibilities in regards to how councils raise taxation and provide local services.

NOTES

1. R. Philpot (ed.) *The Purple Book: A Progressive Future for Labour,* London: Biteback, 2011

Chapter 14

SOCIAL DEMOCRACY AND THE PROGRESSIVE TRADITION

Andrew Vincent

What are the basic intuitions of social democracy? Society is viewed as a mutually supportive, often fragile, arrangement. The social democratic aim is to harmonize – as far as possible – the conditions of social and economic existence. In this scenario the state takes on a fundamental role as planner, enabler and custodian of the common good. The approximate agenda focuses on the *ideal* of full employment; the maintenance of the social rights of citizenship, in the form of guarantees of health and social care; the extension of state-funded public education; the establishment of social minimums, as part of a civilized society; and the desirability of a mixed economy, embodying a mutually beneficial mix of public and private economic enterprises. One additional recurring motif is a distrust of *unregulated* markets as both inefficient and wasteful, creating deep inequalities and insecurities for ordinary citizens. This is not though a mistrust of market as such, only in distinct contexts. This agenda remains a rough-and-ready convention for most social democrats. It is, though, open to all manner of modification in differing circumstances. In Britain, this agenda was the outcome of a subtle blending of ideological elements, particularly those from liberalism and socialism. This ideological hybrid formed a unique concatenation which might be described as 'welfare-based progressivism'.

SOCIAL DEMOCRACY AND HYBRIDITY

The hybrid character of social democracy is its key asset. Although some critics and supporters have fixated on certain elements, such as nationalized industries, this is not essential by any means. If anything social democracy is inherently flexible in terms of policy. What remains striking about it is the commitment to the integuments of a civil and civilized society, focused on maximizing the life chances for as many citizens as possible, however that can be best achieved. Social democracy proposes that a better society is neither simply about wealth creation, nor about achieving some higher moral goal. It can embody aspects of these, but, if it has a core commitment, it is about *enabling* all citizens to live a moderately good life. The economy is seen to exist *for* human beings, not vice versa. Social democracy is thus about providing opportunities for citizens, as well as protecting them from the pitfalls of ill-health and economic distress.

Further, social democracy, because of its hybrid character, is not utopian. It is rather a counsel of imperfection – that is, an attempt to achieve a 'better' society for citizens, not a perfect society. This requires a diverse mix of policies which draw upon markets, states, communities and citizens themselves, without fetishizing any one component. It has no essentialist identity, it is conversely always subject to the pushes and pulls of perspectives.

IDEOLOGICAL COHERENCE AND HISTORICAL DEVELOPMENT

It might be asked: given this hybridity, what held this ideology together, specifically for the post-1945 generation? One reason why social democracy focused so intensively on the state was due to its non-revolutionary character. It saw revolution as leading to authoritarianism and tyranny. It posited conversely the peaceful evolution of polities. Why did this argument on revolution have such a potent effect? To put the matter bluntly, as argued, social democracy was not perfectionist, utopian or indeed positive. It was alternatively backward-looking and oddly negative. It embodied a sober, but realistic, understanding of the possibilities and limits of politics. It is important to reflect here on why so many in the post-1945 generation embraced social democracy so enthusiastically.

The progressive movement, from the late nineteenth century, focused on the following arguments: unregulated capitalism – as well as creating enormous wealth – generated massive inequality, manifest injustices and appalling levels of poverty for large swathes of the populations of European states. This was the vision of urban Britain catalogued meticulously in nineteenth-century government statistical Blue Books, Dickens novels and Booth's and later Rowntree's social surveys. Although there were periodic economic upturns, nonetheless the depressions created a continuous cycle of upheaval and insecurity. For many, violence was the only available option. There were no effective political pathways open to the exploited groups. This state of affairs formed the groundwork for revolution. Such revolutions took many shapes, indeed aspects of early liberalism derived some impetus from such early social ruptures. In the twentieth century the insecurity and distress formed a fertile soil for Marxist-Leninism, Fascism and National Socialism; these were all modernist, extreme authoritarian movements offering rapid answers to social anguish. The overall results of these latter movements cannot easily be gauged. If added together, the levels of utter misery, cruelty and injustice embedded in these multifarious revolutionary moments exceed our grasp. We might summarize this scenario as barbarism *in extremis*.

It is in the above context that we need to consider the development of social democracy. It was not just a normatively driven movement striving for the goals of egalitarianism or social justice. It was also backward-gazing, saying in effect: 'what must we do to prevent this happening again?' and 'what must we do to moderate the effects of economic depression, mass unemployment, social distress and excoriating levels of poverty?' Further, in line with this same logic: 'what must we do to avoid fertilizing, once again, the soil of extreme revolution?' For the generations of the first 60 years of the twentieth century these were not shallow questions. On the contrary, social democracy was a firewall against barbarism. Social democratic states, committed to welfare progressivism, were designed to soften the stark brutalities of social and economic existence. They aimed to redirect states towards the well-being of all their membership and try to meet the yearning for security, stability and moderate prosperity. It was a fine balance, but social democracy did make a courageous and ultimately successful attempt to achieve this aspiration. Indeed it achieved many of its key initial social objectives by the early 1970s, after a long-lasting struggle. By the mid-twentieth century, it embodied the high point of this development of public responsibility. As Ralph Dahrendorf remarked, 'in many respects the social democratic consensus signifies the greatest progress which history has seen so far. Never before have so many people had so many life chances.'[1] Parallel ongoing movements also share a similar ethos. Thus, the establishment of the European Community, the creation of human rights covenants and courts, the subtle transformations of international law, and even the creation of the United Nations by the allied powers, all shared the same substantive aim to avoid the catastrophic events of the early twentieth century being repeated.

SOCIAL DEMOCRACY AND NEO-LIBERALISM

Three things happened to social democracy in the 1970s: first it became the backdrop of everyday life. The struggles that took place to create the social democratic state became submerged within institutional normalcy. New generations appeared who had no memory of this bequest. It became the background expectation, rather than the explicit ideology. Many forgot its rationale. It was gradually replaced by a dull resentment against the tax burdens involved in achieving greater social fairness.

The second issue (which encouraged this tax resentment) was the arrival of a novel proselytizing ideology in the 1980s – developed under the Thatcher–Major–Blair–Brown years. Its ethos was neo-liberalism, although ironically appearing first under the umbrellas of purported conservatism and socialism. Variations of the ideology permeated policy debates. Its basic tenet identified the largely unregulated liberal free market capitalist order as the most efficient allocator of resources. It should not be forgotten that, historically, social democratic thinking had struggled against a largely classical liberal market-based orthodoxy throughout the later nineteenth and early twentieth centuries. The current dominance of neo-liberalism is not though a struggle for economic realities. It is rather one *between* two ideologies. Neo-liberalism, as such, was obsessively concerned with wealth creation, privatization and deregulation; it was individualistic; deeply suspicious of public action; and dedicated to the idea of incessant economic growth. Versions of this ideological argument have saturated Conservative, New Labour and Liberal Democrat policy over the last 30 years.

Third, the aim of social democracy to mollify social and economic animosities – to achieve the laudable aim of a more stable life for all citizens – had unforeseen consequences. One by-product was a distancing of social democracy from ideological debate. Social democracy unwittingly fuelled, in part, an end of ideology. This was a mirage. However, it underpinned a generation who knew little of the history of social democracy. Routine social democratic practice thus generated a public apathy and unawareness of its historical fragility. When economic crises developed in the 1970s, it was social democracy that was (in the minds of this new generation) wholly to blame for not fulfilling the conditions of a good life. Neo-liberalism rushed with glee – and sleight-of-hand – into this vacuum.

The days of enthused proselytism for neo-liberalism are passed. The ideology has submerged deep into institutional vernaculars across the length and breadth of Britain. It has become hegemonic. Despite the 2008 crises of financial services, ideologically it is still the public sector – and the remnants of the social democratic tradition – that are apparently responsible. The banking sector has been ritually chastized, largely for the sake of public perception, and the public sector must pay the *full* price for the inefficiency, waste and irresponsibility fostered by neo-liberal ideology. One can see here the full power of ideological hegemony.

WAYS FORWARD

In current debates about economic austerity or policy priorities, we are encountering ideology head-on. Thus, any return to social democratic themes is a matter of ideological argument. Such a return cannot be countered by fake claims about economic reality. There is no ideology-free economics. What then has social democracy to offer us? Space precludes any detailed suggestions in this chapter; however, the following are indications as to what social democracy can contribute to current debate.

[i] Globalization and the social democratic state

For critics, social democracy cannot be acclimatized to a globalized economy, since it is too attached to an anachronistic vision of the state. For global markets, states are a hindrance. However, for social democracy global corporations are exactly the same economic creatures who inhabited domestic states in the nineteenth and early twentieth centuries, except they are larger and more powerful. Further, the global markets experienced by the majority of the world's population are largely predatory. Globalization rarely benefits humanity, except by accident. Economic gains largely accrue to the global corporations.

Contrary to critics, social democracy is the only ideology that is capable of addressing this problem with insight. It can – ideally with other social democratically inclined states – begin to find constructive ways to negotiate with and ultimately constrain such global corporate interests in the twenty-first century; namely to ensure they contribute fiscally and socially to communities. This is by no means a fantasy. Whilst economic development remains buoyant, criticism of globalization is muted. However, this has not been the case during recent global crises. The logic of this latter point was grasped fully by social democrats in the immediate post-1945 world. A comparable logic – on a much less destructive scale – arose again in 2008–9. This logic is something that social democracy needs to build upon, since it has a clearer and more concrete grasp than any other contemporary ideologies. When markets fail, when unemployment rises, when global banks collapse, when insecurity intensifies, there is no neo-liberal state with *any* solutions, except more of the same.

The only option for dealing with global capitalist markets is via the social democratically inclined state. Despite ideological fanfares to the idea that markets provide cost-effective and efficient solutions, they often fail abysmally and states have to step in. It is not far-fetched to argue that in the same way that early twentieth-century pluralists saw groups or associations as the *corps intermédiare*, standing between individuals and states and protecting human freedoms, that now social democratic states can be the potential *corps intermédiare*, standing between citizens and arbitrary global forces.

[ii] Social democracy and critical state language

In order to achieve this level of state action, there is a need for a conscious reassessment of the language of states. Social democracy, unlike revolutionary or libertarian ideologies, embodies a measured statism, something that can be relearnt. States have clearly failed in the past. The twentieth century shows us how hazardous they can be. Libertarians, anarchists and localists of all stripes all focus on the vices of states. What social democracy enables is a critical reconsideration of the virtues of states. States are not always right, but neither are they always wrong. Social democracy can enable a rebalancing of our current political understanding. With the state we have to be continuously critically aware, without the state we become entirely vulnerable.

There is no simple choice here between an interventionary state and a passive market-based state. This binary should be discarded. A state is always needed to correct markets; individual citizens and groups are required to continuously monitor and assess the state, via democratic procedures. Yet states can and ought to do things that no individual, local community or private company can or would want to do. Maintaining transport infrastructure, policing, judicial systems, education structures, are things that states can do well, if properly financed. Some may fantasize that markets can deal with these without state prompting, but this flies in the face of common sense.

Current debate should not be sidelined here into the cul-de-sac of local autonomy. The localist argument, to date, has neither historical legitimacy nor clear intellectual focus. There have been socialist-inclined movements which emphasized localism and pluralism – that is municipal socialism, guild socialism, trade unionism, and aspects of the co-operative movement, amongst others. However, what is significant about these movements – outside of those that drift into anarchism, syndicalism or romanticized conservative communitarianism – is that they all, to varying degrees, noted their deep vulnerability to powerful corporate interests and the manner in which such interests have always tried to recruit, bully or manipulate the state and legal system for their own ends – and current global corporations are no exception. Such pluralist movements aimed eventually to establish political parties or (minimally) structures, which would enable the state to resist such economic interests for the sake of the common good. Little has changed in this scenario.

There is a clear recognition within social democracy that the state is not a collection of atomized individuals; it is rather an interlaced association involving complex communal interdependences. What social democracy brings to the policy table is a constructive hybridity and flexibility. Its view of the agenda and non-agenda of states has been and should remain open and experimental in character. This is a subtle statist language that we have forgotten over the last 30 years. We need therefore to recover some sense of our own history, over the last century, and thus re-explore and re-engage with the sagacity of the post-1945 generation.

One additional point is that this vision of the social democratic state is not regarded as an alien structure set over citizens. Conversely it is a vessel for enabling citizens to gain the best life chances, in the given circumstances. Further, citizens are seen as critical participants in the state. Social democratic politics should not be about compliance. A social democratic state's authority should be premised on the verve of its *civil* public democratic dialogues. Social democratic statehood needs to be continuously rehabilitated via these public dialogues. The boundaries of such social democratic states are thus largely internal to the dispositions of individual citizens.

[iii] Education

To enable citizens to participate effectively and critically requires a full and rounded process of education. This education should be open to all and not dependent upon an ability to pay. This is the basic logic behind comprehensive schooling and the opening up of universities in the 1950s and 1960s. Again, we should not be diverted by the flaws of previous reforms – policies always need reworking. As long as the basic value aim is to enable all citizens to be able to develop and fulfil their life chances, then it is reasonable for social democratic education policy to evolve.

Universities are an example of an education policy that has been deeply corrupted by reforms of the last few decades. Universities are now, in fact, in a parlous state, particularly as regards genuine education and scholarship. University administrations – rather than teachers – now speak confidently about students as consumers, universities as businesses and education as a global marketing product. Market impacts are seen as valid forms of assessment for academic research. There is a belief that educational quality can be meaningfully measured and judged by this travesty. A good academic now is one who gains more income than others. A good department is one which maximizes external grant income. Students are implicitly encouraged into a life of pure privatized self-interest. The idea that a life could be dedicated to public service is virtually meaningless.

Universities and schools are not alone here. Health services, the civil service and policing are all dominated by the same ideological ethos. None of these can really be either done away with or completely privatized (as neo-liberals would like). None of these practices make profits. There are no shareholders to check management. They have no competitors in any real genuine market sense. And there is no scope for shareholder rebellion if management proves inadequate. They are, by their intrinsic nature, public goods. Only states can actually manage such goods effectively – as the ideology of social democracy grasped.

What we have now is the *worst of markets* coupled with the *worst of public control*. The problem with importing private sector managerial techniques is that it has centralized authority along business lines, but has not at the same time initiated the counterbalances to monitor such managerial authoritarianism. This has created a perverse public sector. It is neither fish nor fowl. In consequence we have largely unaccountable managements trying to redesign public institutions to fit a dogmatic ideologically driven 'strategic vision' and using private sector management techniques to nudge and coerce their staff in an authoritarian manner.

Neo-liberals would, of course, like to acclimatize populations to growing inequality, transforming expectations downwards, so that global competitiveness and profits can be maintained. Some stark choices have to be made here and the full constructive powers of social democracy will have to be called upon in any future government. At baseline, unskilled or semi-skilled labour, in global terms, benefits authoritarian and tyrannical low-wage economies. Do we really want this in Britain? Greater inequality may provide temporary competitive advantages, but in the longer run it will lead to an unravelling of our social fabric, as happened in the nineteenth and early twentieth centuries. Gross inequality, insecurity and violence frequently work in tandem.

The social democratic counterargument is not to level down, but to exploit relative advantages in knowledge. This is not about more employment skills. Skills mutate too rapidly. What is needed is supple and critical citizens who can adjust. Education has a vital role to play here. In social democratic terms, better educated populations not only adapt more effectively, but they are also happier and they lead richer lives. Social democracy offers us a generational chance to do away with the business-orientated, utilitarian, managerial, target-driven and training model of education and to restore the idea of a full, rounded comprehensive vision of equal education for all citizens.

SOCIAL DEMOCRACY AND
THE PROGRESSIVE TRADITION

The prospect of social democracy in government would signal a return to political realism and sanity. Private market-based police, armies, roads, transport networks, education, welfare, prisons, water, or even judicial systems, may look attractive to a minority, but in practice any ordinary rational citizen would know that this latter strategy is verging on ideological psychosis. Social democracy can show us again the meaning and relevance of social provision and its role in enriching citizen's lives.

Social democracy needs to re-establish its links with a broad progressive tradition, a tradition that is confident in our mutual destiny as citizens. In the last two decades many who were purportedly part of the liberal-left of politics have sadly stood outside this rich tradition of welfare progressivism, discarding social democracy and the precious postwar realist legacy for the sake of furtive commitments to neo-liberal values, dressed up in the language of private sector managerialism and – even more obscurely – modernization. Social democracy, on the other hand, is a tradition that rejects the brutality of unregulated global capitalism and the asocial radicalism of neo-liberalism. Labour should once again try to recover and experiment with its flexible social democratic heritage and avoid the siren calls of neo-liberalism and indeed naive visions of localism.

NOTE

1. R. Dahrendorf, 'The End of the Social Democratic Consensus' in *Life Chances*, Chicago: Chicago University Press, 1979; pp.108-9

Chapter 15

LAW AND ORDER

The Challenge for Labour

Helena Kennedy

After the election defeat of 1992, Labour had a serious policy rethink about how to win elections. Labour was anxious to win the trust of middle England and sought to challenge media characterizations that it was full of CND activists who were against war, bleeding hearts who were soft on crime and spendthrifts who would feather-bed the feckless. The party bought the Clinton formula that policy should be developed around winning the swing vote in marginal constituencies. The challenge was to show that Labour too could play hardball. The message had to be that we were as financially astute as the Conservatives; that we could run the military with patriotic robustness and were not afraid of war; and when it came to law and order, it would not be about taking no prisoners but taking lots of prisoners.

It would be too easy to see this shift in policy as a testosterone-driven folly which led to under-regulation of the financial sector, a mad embrace of markets for all purposes, a ratcheting-up of prison numbers, an erosion of civil liberties and a desperate engagement in an illegal disastrous war. However, I think something more complex was taking place.

With the arrival of Thatcher we started to see the slow abandonment of the embedded liberalism that had been a diffuse presence in British politics in the postwar period. There had been shared assumptions across parties about the value of the welfare state and strong public services, about the necessary independence of the civil service, about protecting the special role of the judiciary, maintaining safeguards for those accused of crime and imprisoning only as a last resort. Cultural shifts take time but this pull away from those tenets is now coming into stark relief, often in cruel and destructive ways. Friedrich Hayek's theories about the market and liberal economics had been absorbed deep into the political bloodstream. Political think tanks, government departments and even some of the universities' faculties had been successfully penetrated by lobbying outfits with large purses, which urged market philosophy into every aspect of our lives; any idea of reversing the Thatcher pendulum of privatization and the marketizing of public services was abandoned by New Labour as going against the prevailing tide. It was even accelerated in important areas.

New Labour's warm embrace of the market and its endeavour to thin out the role of the state in the delivery of public services and welfare called upon it to chart new waters. Unfortunately, when Labour politicians do that they too often slide into right-of-centre positions rather than progressive ones – this was particularly evident with law and order. Modernizing our institutions and social constructions is a vital role for a reforming government, but it is always important to remain true to your core values as a party. That was the piece New Labour forgot. In an effort to engage all sections of the public, New Labour colonized conservative policies on crime and punishment.

Overall New Labour's story on law is not a good one. Labour got itself into a terrible mess when confronted with the horror of 9/11 and the threat of international terrorism. Its desire to be a good ally and friend to the United States led it into desperately wrong policy decisions. It is always a temptation for Labour in government to be in thrall to the security services, desperate for approval from this most unaccountable part of the state apparatus rather than controlling it. We should have learned from the painful experiences of dealing with Northern Ireland that locking people up without trial only feeds a powerful sense of injustice in the sections of the community which feels under suspicion of links with the terrorist threat. Internment of any kind always operates as a driver for recruitment. It did for the IRA and has done for Al Qaeda.

Standing in a court and listening to a Labour Attorney General argue against a prohibition on the use of evidence that may have emanated from torture was not an edifying moment in Labour's history. The whole effort to lock up suspects for 90 days without charge should remain a source of shame to all involved. Despite the retreat that was forced on Tony Blair over this serious assault on civil liberty, what was extraordinary was that Gordon Brown was somehow persuaded to revisit the same terrain, calling for detention for 42 days without charge when he was prime minister. Nowhere in the developed world is such detention considered acceptable.

But there was worse. The supreme test of our commitment to law was in relation to the invasion of Iraq; this was where we lost all moral courage. Contorting the law to support going to war in Iraq, rather than genuinely following advice that doing so would contravene international law, was probably the lowest point of the Labour administration's abuse of law. It remains a weeping sore. It led to considerable loss of life of our own military personnel and of innocent Iraqi civilians. The cost internationally has been grievous and it fed the very terrorism it was supposed to combat. The idea that war must only ever be a last resort was abandoned for spurious reasons.

The catalogue of horrors brought on by disproportionate responses to the terrorist threat has been long and damaging to the rule of law and human rights. We have seen the invention of control orders, a form of house arrest and sometimes even internal exile, which the courts had to step in and modify to make conform to some modicum of humanity. There has been compelling evidence of the UK colluding in the United States policy of rendition, whereby the torture of prisoners was outsourced to countries which are proudly expert in cruel and violent interrogation practices. All these things were done on New Labour's watch and on occasion Labour ministers signed off on shameful conduct as is alleged to have happened with regard to Libyans rendered to Gaddafi. Getting back on track is impossible without acknowledging how bad it got. It is not good enough to wait for inquiries decades after the event and for prime ministers then to apologize for the behaviour of our forces or security services, as we have just seen with Bloody Sunday or the murder of the solicitor Patrick Finucane in Northern Ireland during the Troubles.

We must not repeat the same mistakes or fashion our law and order policies out of the same cloth. Law matters.

But departures from decent standards were not just in response to terrorism. The story on sentencing of offenders has been shameful. Our prisons are full to bursting and Britain now tops Europe's league table for the highest proportion of citizens incarcerated. This was due in large part to New Labour home secretaries conscientiously adopting policies that left no space to their right for the Tories to occupy. The bid to outsmart our opponents and cosy up to right-wing tabloid press became more important than doing what was just. The invention of the Anti-Social Behaviour Order led to a huge increase in young people going to jail simply because they breached an order by wandering into streets that were off limits. The reason the prisons are so full is because sentences have been greatly lengthened. Our home secretaries engaged in a hectoring rhetoric, which made it hard for the courts to do anything other than jail people. Judicial discretion was reduced and the American 'three strikes and you're out' style of automatic response was introduced, along with indeterminate sentences.

We now lock up people who should not be in jail, many with addiction problems or mental illness. The statistics in relation to women are stark. The numbers of women in prison more than doubled under New Labour and although Baroness Jean Corston, the Labour peer, wrote a powerful report advising reform, far too little was done. The statistics: 63% of women in prison have committed non-violent offences; 81% have experienced domestic violence or childhood sexual abuse; 70% have more than one diagnosed mental condition; 68% have been involved in drink or drugs abuse.

One of the shocking things to watch recently was John Reid in the House of Lords roasting the government over the plans of the Conservative Justice Secretary, Ken Clarke, to reduce the prison population. He ranted about turning criminals onto the streets. We used to be the party with sensible measured policies on crime. We used to be the people who understood that most offending has its roots in serious social problems and that what is needed is community programmes to address those ills. This is what helps victims of crime most effectively.

We really lost our way.

Labour repeatedly attempted to reduce trial by jury – one of the best elements in the UK system of justice. First, Jack Straw claimed it should be kept only for serious crime and taken away from lesser matters; then it was to be removed from fraud and terrorism as being beyond the capacity of mere citizens. The reforms were only resisted by strong opposition in the Lords. Juries are the democratic element in the system – lending it democratic legitimacy – and if any party should be promoting juries it should be Labour.

David Blunkett got it into his head that too many people were being acquitted because the middle classes found excuses to avoid jury service. In conversations in America he discovered that everyone there can be summoned, including judges and policemen. He immediately introduced changes which allow the same here. What he did not realize is that in the USA there is substantial challenge by lawyers to potential jurors through a system called 'voir dire'. The potential juror can be questioned as to their job and attitudes to politics and crime and be asked to stand down by the prosecution or the defence if they are unhappy with the replies. No policeman sits on a criminal case. No criminal judge sits on a criminal case. This interrogation of jurors is allowed because a juror with insider knowledge can bring it to bear on a case in questionable ways. They may be predisposed to one side or the other because their role in the police or on the bench may instinctively affect their view of the evidence. Or they may even succumb to their usual function within the jury room – playing detective or judge. The mere possibility that this could happen should militate against officials within the justice system sitting on juries. We have abolished the right to challenge jurors in the UK unless they actually know a party to the case. So we now have judges who normally try cases sitting on juries and policemen from the murder squad trying murders at the Old Bailey. These are roles which are part of the system and it is unbelievable that those fulfilling them should be asked to move across the courtroom metaphorically and sit in judgement. David Blunkett was a good education minister but was a menace in the Home Office.

Thankfully, Ed Miliband has taken Labour to a new place on many policy issues. He has been prepared rightly to admit that New Labour got some things wrong. However, there has been no significant shift on the law and order front; the fear of being accused by the tabloid press of being soft on crime remains. We see it with the old guard coming out against Theresa May's decision not to extradite Gary McKinnon, the computer hacker who was wanted by the Americans for hacking into the Pentagon's computers but who suffers from an extreme case of Asperger's syndrome. It was accepted that he had no espionage intent but did it because of his obsessive personality. Instead of welcoming a display of compassion and sensible use of the Human Rights Act, she was excoriated by some of our number.

We also had Labour recently abstaining in the House of Lords when the Coalition introduced their 'Shoot a Burglar' policy. This is a proposal to allow disproportionate force in defending yourself if someone trespasses into your home. But the law as it stands allows a person to respond with force, even if excessive, if it is felt necessary to the householder at the time. Self-defence acknowledges that it is not always possible to measure to a nicety what would be proportionate. This change is in total contravention of the Human Rights Act and New Labour in government accepted the advice of the Joint Committee on Human Rights not to go down that road. Yet our shadow ministers gave instructions to the whips to abstain in the vote because of how it would appear in the press. Some of us in the House of Lords ignore such madness but why are we incapable of taking the arguments to the public? When I speak at public meetings I find the public listen to sensible explanations about the law and, although they may start out with punitive views, soon accept the arguments for alternatives to prison.

Labour has also been officially resisting prisoners having voting rights – even if it is only those on the shortest of sentences for non-violent crimes who need be given the right. This means we are breaking the law. We signed a Convention that said we would comply with European Court rulings, yet here we are willing to tear up the rule of law. It puts us on the same side as people who want to decouple us from the European Court of Human Rights. It sends out appalling signals to people like Putin about breaching law when we don't like it and is a disgraceful precedent. And all because we fear the tabloids.

For some who were in the New Labour government it is impossible to say that they did not make Faustian pacts. They still cannot accept that the Iraq war was an egregious wrong. Many still refuse to accept that their efforts to keep business on side led them into treacherous alliances and meant they failed to hold the world of high finance in check. They still cannot accept that some of their policies in health and education opened the doors to what is now happening under a government of a very different stripe. As a party, Labour has to have a serious rethink.

Part of the problem is that those who come to government always see themselves as the good guys. 'So what is all this old-hat business about the malign power of the state? People who share our values, should know that we would not use our power to bad ends. Trust us.' And while I think our guys are by and large good guys, I also know that there must always be serious restraints on power in place.

Once people 'are the state' or have their hands on the levers of the state they often forget the basic lessons that safeguards and legal protections are there for the possible bad times which could confront us, when a government may be less hospitable, or when social pressures make law our only lifeline. Governments ignore the fact that once a welfare benefit has been removed or liberties have been lost they are almost impossible to restore. The idea of there now being a benign state is a contemporary myth.

In his own writings on politics David Blunkett, the former home secretary, presses this delusion. The state, he told us in the *Guardian* on Saturday 14 September 2002, is not some bogey of which we should be afraid. It is in fact you and me, the community:

> I still find it surprising that so many people who consider themselves to be on the left of the political spectrum find themselves instinctively aggressive about the role of the state and insist on their absolute protection against it. Those of us on the centre left must remember that the state can be a positive force, empowering and enabling people to shape their lives, a collective vehicle to achieve progressive change.

Civil liberties, he says, are as much about the needs of citizens to be protected from crime and to live in security as about the civil liberties of a person accused. And of course he is right, but he is only partly right. The welfare state provided my family with housing as I was growing up, made it possible for me to have a higher education without paying fees and with a grant, and it then provided wonderful care for my elderly mother in Scotland in her last years. People in the United Kingdom today are not so lucky. Many of us regret that those life-enhancing opportunities made possible by progressive politics are no longer available for all but a very few.

We can see the positive role that can be played by the state in the hands of visionary politicians – providing support and security as well as guarding our human rights. We agree that we must be protected from the predations of criminals. The state should prosecute wrongs with vigour but state power must also be kept in check and it often falls to the courts to do that. The police, the security services, prison guards and others can and do abuse their powers. When politicians say 'trust us' they usually speak in good faith but we should always exercise caution. We have to be sure that such trust is justified and not being sought to capture easy public approval.

In New Labour's 'post-state' vision, criminal justice looked like another aspect of state provision, ripe for rebalancing, giving more power to the consumer, identified as the victim. The problem with that analysis is that the accused is also a consumer of the criminal justice system. Since the criminal justice system is a 'social good' belonging to us all, taking over the prosecution of crime in the interests of us all, it does not lend itself to the 'customer' analogies. The rhetoric of 'rebalancing the system' as between victims and the accused disingenuously presents the criminal trial as a contest between these two parties, thus denying the central role of the state. Giving more power to the victim has too often really involved giving more power to the state. Every erosion of liberty or removal of a safeguard was justified on the basis that it will help victims. Yet how is the victim advantaged if reductions in the protection for an accused lead to wrongful convictions? Convicting the wrong person or convicting someone unjustly is a sour kind of justice. This may not have been the original design, but these are the distortions which take place if reform is embarked upon without consideration of wider consequences. Successful reform is not possible without seeing that there are qualitative differences between substantive reform, which goes to the founding principles of the law, and process reform, which is about procedural change. The former can have disturbing implications for other parts of our carefully knit checks and balances and should be undertaken only with caution; the latter are of less consequence. But Labour ministers often proceeded as if there was no difference between the two.

It is really important that Labour is seen as the champion of the rule of law. What does that mean? It means that there should be a clear recognition that no nation can survive without just laws and adherence to them. The rule of law is one of the tools we use in our stumbling progress towards civilizing the human condition: a structure of law, with proper methods and independent judges, before whom even a government must be answerable. It is the only restraint upon the tendency of power to debase its holders. History is dogged by the tragic fact that whenever individuals, political parties or countries become too powerful there is a temptation to refuse to subordinate that power to wider and higher law. We have seen it recently with the United States picking and choosing when to apply the Geneva Convention.

The important thing for all of us to remember is that the rule of law is not simply what a government says it is: obeying rules that you have formulated yourself is no great discipline. As we know from observing Russia and China, the rule *of* law is not the same as rule *by* law.

Any modern conception of the rule of law includes human rights protections and safeguards of civil liberties. The judiciary is a vital component in this and independence of the judiciary has to be maintained with vigour – even when the decisions do not go the way we like. The right method for challenge to judgements is through the courts. Maintaining this respect also sends out vital messages to our own communities and around the world about our value system. It was appalling to hear Labour government ministers go to war on judges who ruled that their policies contravened human rights – for example, where refused asylum seekers had all benefits withdrawn and the courts decided that leaving people destitute was inhumane.

One of the greatest achievements of Labour in government was the incorporation of the European Convention of Human Rights into domestic law. The Human Rights Act (and the Scotland Act which does the same north of the border) brought the European Convention home. It had actually been drafted by UK lawyers after the Second World War and it drew upon our own common law traditions of protecting civil liberties and holding fair trial processes. Labour should be saying that loudly and clearly. Labour sometimes forgets that most of our civil liberties came about because ordinary men and women in the United Kingdom fought for them. They were challenges to the abuse of power by elites and are a fundamental prerequisite for truly democratic government.

The idea that Conservatives should be the champions of civil liberties is surreal. Collective memory about abuse of power, from the Tolpuddle Martyrs, the early trade unionists of 1836, to the use of 'Suspected Persons' laws against black people in the 1960s and 1970s, fired a belief in most people on the Left that civil liberties mattered. But knowing elementary things about why, where and when have become rare virtues. Knowledge gives us the power to say 'no' and the ability to give reasons for the rejection. If we do not understand past struggle we are much more likely to be taken in by new-fangled dogma. In order to revise you need to know something about what went before. In order to renew effectively, you need to understand the old. If the urgently evanescent – tomorrow's headline, the next poll or the next vote – is all that matters, discernment drops away.

The amnesiac loses direction. It is in these spaces that charlatans can peddle their wares.

What we should have learned from history is that, in the long run, abuses by the state are far more dangerous to liberty and democracy than individual criminal conduct – as dangerous and disturbing as that is.

Labour must be at the forefront of preserving the Human Rights Act, its own legislative child, and it should fight with vigour any attempt to break away from the European Court of Human Rights. The court has led the way in the world showing that human rights can be protected through law and across different legal systems. It is being sorely tested now because so many former Soviet countries have joined the Council of Europe and, since they have such a shallow hold on human rights, they are constantly being found in breach of the European Convention of Human Rights. There is a large backlog of cases and people like Putin do not like being brought to book. If we in Britain refuse to respond positively to court rulings how do we imagine Russia or Moldova will respond?

Of course, there are occasions when the court gets it wrong. No court ever gets it right all of the time. Our own courts have needed reform at different times over the years, but if the UK were to de-couple from the European system, as many Conservatives would want, we would lose all moral authority in the world as a nation that stands for the protection of human rights. That is why it was quite wrong for us to refuse to put in place some reform on prisoners' votes. The European Court was only objecting to our having a blanket ban on prisoners being able to vote. Blanket bans have a bad history. Governments have been known to imprison people to remove them from the franchise and blanket bans against whole categories of peoples have worked against minorities such as Jews, Roma and homosexuals. All that was expected of us was that we gave a postal vote to some of the prison population. The reason we did not was that we thought it would play badly in the press in the run-up to an election.

Over the last 30 years we have seen the increased politicization of criminal justice. In every election, crime now emerges as a crucial political issue and it has become very difficult to inject any sanity into the debates. Yet entering a Dutch auction with the other political parties over who has the tougher policies is unsustainable; it is also an unworthy endeavour for Labour, especially if it involves eroding rights and civil liberties and fails to engage with productive ways to reduce criminal behaviour and provide alternatives to prison wherever appropriate. Labour's position should be clear. Serious crime needs a serious response and prison is the appropriate place for people who are a danger to the public, but large-scale incarceration is not only economic madness, it is the best way of making people truly criminal.

Part IV

SOCIALIST INTERNATIONALISM

Chapter 16

AN ETHICAL FOREIGN POLICY?

Peter Kilfoyle

Robin Cook was well known as a knowledgeable racing fan, with a keen eye for a winner. Yet he would not have offered odds on the furore that his first speech as foreign secretary, back in May 1997, was to cause by the inclusion of a seemingly unexceptional line: 'our foreign policy must have an ethical dimension'.

Speaking to an audience of diplomats and journalists in the grandeur of the Locarno Room in the Foreign Office, he simply stated what had been discussed in political and diplomatic circles for decades. In fact, Cook had set out four other goals of British policy before using the phrase 'an ethical dimension' as an introduction to a passage on democratic and human rights, emphasizing them as central to the Blair government's foreign policy.

Many seized upon this as naive; and those conflicting views were to find early expression in a widespread debate over the sale of Hawk jets to the Indonesian dictator Suharto. It was alleged that these were being used in a ground attack role in East Timor. Cook held that existing contracts – the Hawk deal having been agreed by John Major's government – must be honoured. Nevertheless, it was an early indication of the difficulties of counterposing ethics, however conditionally, to the traditional pragmatism of British foreign policy.

Although we cannot stress too much the distortion by commentators of Cook's presentation (he himself was careful to recognize the limitations of what might be achieved), he was adamant that pragmatism and self-interest alone ought not to be the only guiding lights to British foreign policy – his mission statement supplied 'an ethical content to foreign policy and recognizes that the national interest cannot be defined only by narrow realpolitik'.[1]

However, the phrase 'ethical foreign policy' stuck in the public's mind, and even more so with lazy political commentators with limited research skills. After all, although Cook had never used the phrase, it was a concept which went back decades in those Western circles concerned with such esoteric policy discussions. Dean Rusk, for example, would utter platitudes about ethics and morals in his approach to foreign policy on one occasion; dismiss their relevance as nonsense on another. Perhaps the British were more sophisticated in their approach to foreign policy formulation; but in truth, it was a series of changes, international shifts and innovations which led us to our present discussions, not inspired individuals. Governments are now having to face wider demands for accountability and transparency than ever before. This has been paralleled by both increased domestic and international pressure for responsibility in their dealings abroad. The United Kingdom has been no exception to these global trends.

The postwar establishment of such NGOs as Amnesty International, Human Rights Watch and the International Commission of Jurists has been critical in the promotion of the consideration of an ethical dimension to foreign policy, as we now also contend with a whole raft of international agreements which did not exist until after the Second World War. The whole process of accommodation to new realities has been accelerated since the end of the Cold War, allowing a new opportunity to refocus foreign policy in most countries in line with those rapidly changing global circumstances.

Before looking objectively at those changed circumstances, it would be sensible to look at what precisely is meant by an ethical dimension to foreign policy. Cook linked it to support for 'demands of other peoples for the democratic rights on which we insist for ourselves', with 'human rights at the heart of our foreign policy'. It does not mean we must abandon the trading and commercial dimensions of foreign policy, nor the defence element. It is meant to inform decisions in those areas with a notion of international citizenship piloted by Australian foreign minister Gareth Evans in the Hawke and Keating governments.

Naturally, in such circumstances there would be very difficult decisions to be made, although that might be easier today than it was as recently as 20 years ago. For example, important advances have been made in the limitations of arms sales – landmines is one case in point – whereby the case is now generally accepted that the indiscriminate nature of such weapons means that they can no longer be justified as a legitimate arms export. Likewise, the United Kingdom Military Training Scheme now emphasizes human rights awareness, and civilian accountability, of the military personnel being trained.

There has also been a massive shift in British government thinking, signalled by the establishment of the Department for International Development (DfID). Not only has DfID shown efficiency and flexibility since its release from the control of the Foreign and Commonwealth Office, but the departmental separation of aid from trade has enabled better targeting of aid for the relief of poverty and promotion of development. It has also removed a degree of featherbedding from exporters who were being given a free ride on the back of our aid programme.

Unfortunately, as with any policy, politicians can distort the intentions behind it; and foreign policy with an ethical dimension has been no exception. Human rights arguments have been put forward for a whole series of military actions since Cook's speech – Kosovo, Sierra Leone, Iraq, Libya and the long war in Afghanistan – in order to assuage doubtful domestic audiences who are increasingly critical of foreign adventures. War, it can be said, is diplomacy by another name (apologies to Clausewitz). If so, many reject that thinking. Thus, large numbers of British people have become extremely cynical about spiel invoking human rights to justify military action, making it ever more difficult – given perceived government duplicity – to marshal popular support for any action at all.

Disillusion has meant that in the UK, Europe and the United States, there has been withdrawal from engagement even in those areas where an ethical case can be made for some degree of intervention. Public distrust of government intentions, together with a regular parade of body bags, are powerful disincentives to a proactive foreign policy in critical areas.

Yet there are successes, particularly in those 'softer' areas of foreign policy which require support. However, we must first recognize where we are as a nation. We are a medium-sized nation on the fringe of Europe. We have been – and continue to be – in decline economically and militarily. Despite domestic claims, we are peripheral to Europe and less important than Poland (missile bases) and Israel (domestic politics) to the United States, itself a nation in decline, but still the only global military superpower. So much for the much-vaunted 'special relationship' – special to whom, and when? Our trading base has shrunk as has our manufacturing capacity. Our main attraction to people overseas often seems to be as a large heritage park. Our diplomatic presence has shrunk in many parts of the world (often being replaced by an expanding Chinese presence).

Notwithstanding this rather sobering picture, we still have reserves of democratic, legal and cultural capital. Our language is the global language. We have strong ties in all continents and a degree of social cohesion and educational provision which is the envy of many. Although shaken by recent events, we are still a global financial player, and a nation respected within many international organizations. How do we build upon these advantages through our foreign policy? How do we do so with an ethical dimension? What ought we to foster and what ought we to jettison?

Labour's current 'Britain in the World' policy commission continues its 2012 programme with a case-by-case review of current issues. For example, in March, it considered the human rights situation in Colombia. There is no doubt about the appalling human rights situation in Colombia; but this consideration of Colombia appears to be a response to the intense and successful pressure of the Justice for Colombia group, rather than to an a priori review of the place of human rights across the whole range of foreign policy issues. Such a review might then illustrate how we can accommodate our enlightened self-interest to the centrality of human rights in our foreign policy thinking. Let us take Israel as an example.

We as a nation were a key to the establishment of the state of Israel; and we consequently have a particular responsibility for the Palestinian people who were disenfranchised and displaced. The conflict between Israel and the Palestinians is also recognized as key to stability in the Middle East. Such stability is in turn critical to Western energy supplies and our own prosperity.

Unfortunately, we are seen by many in the Arab world as tied in to American policy in this area. American policy has its own failings, as set out by Mearsheimer and Walt[2] – it is hamstrung by the Israeli influence on American domestic politics. One can see the electoral constraints on American presidents and their resultant dilemma. There is no comparable domestic political pressure on the British government. Nor do cosmetic exercises like the Blair initiative on behalf of the Quartet change the perception of the United Kingdom as, at best equivocal on Palestinian rights and, at worst, an American/Israeli poodle.

A genuinely independent British policy pushing harder on the rights of Palestinians might alienate the American Israeli lobby and the hard Right in Israel itself, but it would undoubtedly win us countless friends across the Arab and Muslim world, whilst being ethical in itself. Naturally, we would support the security guarantees for Israel itself, but within parameters set by the international community rather than those set by the ultra-right wing in the Knesset.

Such an ethical stand might even help our American friends to see a way out of their own impasse in the Middle East, given the grip that lobby groups like AIPAC have on both the Republican and Democrat policy stance. Moral leadership can, on occasion, sway the mightiest of powers in the world, shining a light on truths to which those powers sometimes seem blind.

It is also the case that American policy is not necessarily in accord with British interests or motives. Ever since the Suez debacle, British governments have, by and large, striven to be in line with American foreign policy. In part, this was due to our economic dependence on American goodwill. When Harold Wilson refused to commit troops to Vietnam, his government paid an economic price. This is no longer the case, although our involvement in Afghanistan and Iraq (particularly Iraq) reflected our willingness to provide diplomatic and political cover for essentially American wars.

Interestingly, in these days of diminishing defence capacity, British efforts in both Basra and Helmand were seen by the Americans as less than effective – in both cases, British forces were stiffened by American units. It was not so much our military input that mattered, as much as our usefulness as a political and diplomatic counterweight to critics of American adventurism.

However, even a slight distancing from our current posture begs the question: where do we go? We actually go nowhere. We stay where we are – a part of Europe. Continental Europe remains our biggest trading partner. We are culturally, geographically and politically (through the European Union) part of Europe. Through NATO, we are tied in to the bulk of Europe in a military alliance, although this alliance needs to be updated, given that the original targets of its forces – the USSR and the Warsaw Pact – no longer exist. Notwithstanding Europhobes in the United Kingdom, it would appear entirely logical that a wholehearted commitment to Europe as the centre of our policy is unarguable.

This does not undermine our interests in the rest of the world; nor deny an ethical dimension to our policies. *Au contraire*, if we truly believe that unity is strength, we might exercise our influence through the medium of a Europe which – despite its current economic difficulties – will remain a major force in the world, at least economically. British influence might very well be just the catalyst to give Europe the diplomatic and ethical edge it needs.

As we have withdrawn from empire since the Second World War, other countries have filled the vacuum we have left behind. Thus, we have little presence on the Pacific Rim, and our voice in Africa is more muted than it was. China has expanded vigorously, economically and diplomatically; and they and other Asian Tigers roam those parts of the world we once dominated. We remain an island on the edge of Europe, and on the shores of the Atlantic. We remain a gateway for Europe to the Americas, and we are linked to the rest of the globe by sea and air. Trade is once more the key to British prosperity, and friendly foreign relations are invaluable to British trade interests.

Does that include a linkage between trade and aid? It is certainly true that trade between even the most disadvantaged Third World nations and the developed world has its advantages for both parties. Yet there are circumstances whereby unfettered aid is the only way in which human catastrophe can be avoided. For example, whilst we wish to see the Horn of Africa developed over time to be self-sustaining, problems such as overwhelming drought, or the depredations of violence in Somalia or South Sudan, demand instant aid to sustain blameless populations.

Our Department of International Development has been very successful since 1997. Its successes have had the by-product of 'soft' credit for UK plc. This is not a bad thing of itself. However, we must not seek to engineer commercial advantage out of human tragedy for its own sake. That would not only be unethical, but counterproductive over time in terms of our national reputation.

For foreign policy to be successful, it requires continuity amongst other things. Neat political cycles of four or five years rarely accord with the demands of international relations. An ethical dimension to our foreign policy is even more difficult to maintain unless it is embedded in the culture and thinking of the Foreign and

Commonwealth Office, the responsibility of which for foreign policy transcends the demands of any one government. Indeed, it is difficult for any single government to change conventional foreign policy against the current of longer-term contemporary wisdom on any given subject.

We have already mentioned international aid – it is now a given responsibility of governments of all political hues. It is fair to anticipate that climate change will increasingly be another such area of common ground, with all of its concomitant challenges to ethical thinking. Almost since the birth of the nuclear age, all governments have been endeavouring to remove weapons of mass destruction from the world's armouries. These efforts will continue, and rightly so. However, there are still battles to be fought in convincing the electorate in our democracy that international aid is in the interests of us all, as well as being right in it; that climate change is real, and needs to be combated internationally; and that nuclear weapons are in no one's interests, despite the claimed success of MAD (mutual assured destruction) theory.

There are messages which need to be taken on behalf of our country to the rest of the world. They need a medium through which those messages go. Obviously, we have our embassies and legations throughout the world. Whether we *need* such a massive presence in such attractive locations as the European capitals, or the various American outposts, is highly debatable, particularly as we have closed down our immediate presence in many Third World countries. The BBC through the World Service remains a key source of our British story, as does the British Council. Their exercise of 'soft' power via British culture, with all of its traditional virtues and strengths, is surely vital to maintaining a disproportionately effective British voice in international affairs.

For that presence to survive means avoiding putting too many of our foreign policy eggs in a weakening American basket. For the foreseeable future, the United States will remain the world's only military superpower, and it is sensible for us to be on side with them. However, it is inevitable that an American military decline will eventually match an economic decline relative to the new, rising economies of China and India, and the further competition of Brazil and Russia.

This would indeed be a brave new world with a more introspective United States, and competing economic giants in search of resources and markets in parts of the globe where British interests are already a threatened species. Contemporaneously, Australia and New Zealand will continue to intensify their involvement with Asia, as Canada and the USA become ever more interdependent. With the old Commonwealth striking their own courses, and the new commonwealth ambiguous at best, we are left with the obvious berth on the good ship Europe.

A secure 'home' within Europe gives us the secure base from which to propagate the values which give our own polity its distinctive features – stability, tolerance, equity, amongst others. Add to these our commitment to human rights in our dealing with other nations, and our separation of aid from trade, and we have a framework within which foreign policy can be developed in an ethical context. We have the machinery with which to deliver our 'soft' objectives – a first-rate diplomatic corps and its trade offshoots; the British Council; and the BBC World Service. All that we need is the will to recognize that we are able to provide a template for others to follow. To do so, we must move out of a comfort zone which we have inhabited for over 60 years. The world has moved on substantially in that time; so must British foreign policy.

NOTES

1. Robin Cook speech, 12 May 1997
2. J.J. Mearsheimer and S.M. Walt, *The Israel Lobby and US Foreign Policy*, London: Allen Lane, 2007

Chapter 17

A PROGRESSIVE INTERNATIONALIST ANSWER TO A PERFECT STORM

Peter Hain MP

Indiscriminate threats to the whole planet, mainly through global warming and climate change, mean there is now a danger of a 'perfect storm', with every country affected. On top of the challenges of poverty, terrorism, conflict, war, cyber attacks and proliferation of weapons of mass destruction, this 'perfect storm' means Britain's future international policy needs to be entirely recast, with traditional approaches to 'foreign policy' redundant.

Food and water supplies are under acute pressure from a burgeoning global population, currently just over 7 billion but growing by 200,000 people per day to an estimated 9 billion by 2050.

Rocketing food prices and an exponential increase in the demand for food, especially in China and India, means food security is a major problem – and not simply for the near a billion people undernourished or starving. Food reserves are at a 50-year low and rising demand seems insatiable.

In China, for instance, urbanization and a rapidly growing middle class have seen a radical change in dietary preferences, with a fall in traditional staples such as rice and corn and a massive rise in meat consumption. The consumption of more water-intensive fruits and vegetables, now the largest part of the average Chinese diet, has more than quadrupled since the early 1960s. Meat, fruit and vegetables require much more land and water to produce than cereal crops. And over 12 times the quantity of water is required to produce the equivalent amount of beef as rice and wheat.

Consequently, food and water security are inextricably linked. In Sub-Saharan Africa alone, 40% of the population, or 330 million people, have no accessible decent water, a plight affecting nearly 900 million people across the world. To get water, more than 1 billion people make a three-hour journey on foot, and over one-third of the world's population live in a water-scarce region. As societies urbanize and industrialize, modern lifestyles require huge additional amounts of water which is in turn a potential source of conflict: it would not be a surprise to see 'water wars' in future.

The world will require 50% more food and water by 2030 and the same amount of extra energy – in part to source the extra food and water. And acute energy shortages coupled with extreme volatility in fuel costs – oil prices very high and forecast to remain very high – is another source of the 'perfect storm', with civil unrest and mass migration northwards from the Southern Hemisphere also likely.

Such intractable international problems defy traditional diplomatic solutions. For instance, climate change followed by the destruction of rain forests is in turn driven by rising global consumption and market forces. The global banking crisis of 2007–8 was triggered by worldwide contagion from 'sub-prime' mortgages in America. It gridlocked private credit and investment, and massively cut Western government spending and investment, triggering a financial development crisis. Apart from the UK under the last Labour government, most G8 countries have failed to meet their 2005 Gleneagles commitment to double aid to Africa, with the UN stating that there is a financing gap of up to $200 billion needed from developed countries to achieve its Millennium Development Goals in 2015.

Just as all these challenges require multilateral, inter-governmental responses, so 'foreign policy' is now inextricably intertwined with 'domestic' policy. How effective could a domestic government campaign against HIV/AIDS be when in 2000 three-quarters of British sufferers were infected whilst travelling in Africa? How can one country prevent a handful of students, as occurred in the Philippines in 2000, sending out a virus capable of disabling 10 million computers worldwide? How can we mobilize against global warming or illegal drug use and their deadly affects, when the cause is not some hostile power's ambition or greed, but millions of individual decisions mainly by Western consumers?

The challenges we face as a nation over the coming decades will not be confined by nation-state boundaries. The main threats to our economy, our security, our health and our general well-being will be global in both origin and impact. A major global flu pandemic could cause global economic losses of $1 trillion due to knock-on macroeconomic effects. Migration – with 200 million people (the size of Brazil) now on the move globally every year – places huge strains on the entire domestic agenda from jobs, to housing to race relations. The pensions of European workers are likely to depend in part on investments made in fast growing economies such as China and India.

The problems are joined up, so government must be joined up. Previously, responsibility for foreign policy resided in an elite group of specialist diplomats. But tensions arising from declining water tables in the Middle East, collapsing fish stocks in the Atlantic and persistent drought in East Africa cannot be solved at a summit. The task requires the specialized skills of all government departments – and the committed and innovative involvement of non-government actors in business and civil society.

Successful international policy will in future centre on 'convergent' policy solutions by joined-up governments forming new partnerships both domestically and globally. As the concept of 'foreign' becomes ever-harder to define, we should re-badge the British Foreign Office the Global Affairs Office, and give it a Treasury-type reach into every Whitehall Department with each required to agree its own 'convergence programme'.

Britain under Labour should lead a process to end traditional foreign policy and to evolve a new foreign policy based upon global linkages and embracing global responsibility; a foreign policy for a world in which there is no longer any such place as 'abroad'.

GLOBALIZATION AND INTERDEPENDENCY

Our growing interdependency is self-evident. Only collective action globally will be able to deal with 'the perfect storm'.

Some on the Left suggest that we should adopt a Canute posture, trying to halt the rising tide of globalization, while some on the Right are happy to take its economic benefits, but not the social responsibility that goes with it. The Right – with its prejudice for nationalism, protectionism and unilateralism – offers only simple responses to complex problems, because reliance on free markets and national self-interest is incapable of producing the necessary response when the threats are global and universal.

Only the progressive Left – with our belief in internationalism not isolationism, and multilateralism not unilateralism – can meet the challenges of globalization.

The failure of the neo-conservatives like George W. Bush to grasp this essential truth in the end undermined even his major obsession – global support for the fight against international terrorism. In stark contrast there was a bipartisan US project on national security published in autumn 2006 – chaired by President Clinton's former national security adviser, Tony Lake, and President Reagan's former Secretary of State, George Shultz. Entitled *Forging a World of Liberty Under Law*, it rightly acknowledged: 'power cannot be wielded unilaterally, and in the pursuit of a narrowly drawn definition of the national interest, because such actions breed growing resentment, fear, and resistance.'

Labour is well placed to provide leadership, drawing on the party's internationalist tradition: the passionate Europeanism of Roy Hattersley and John Smith; the unflinching Atlanticism of Ernie Bevin and Denis Healey; the unyielding support of anti-colonial struggles by Fenner Brockway and Michael Foot; and the courage of Jack Jones and George Orwell fighting fascism in the Spanish Civil War.

In our increasingly interdependent world, marrying that internationalist heritage to the progressive goals of the future is more important than ever: recognizing that common interests and common problems can only be solved by collective action; that global stability depends upon global justice; and that we must maintain the Left's historic duty to defend human rights and promote democracy around the world.

STRONGER INTERNATIONAL INSTITUTIONS

Just as the challenges presented by globalization will frequently come from beyond our own borders, so too will the solutions. That's why international institutions and respect for common international rules are more crucial than ever.

With our place on the UN Security Council, and our membership of the European Union, G8, NATO, the Commonwealth, IMF, World Bank and the World Trade Organization, Britain is well placed to lead the imperative for effective, global multilateralism by influencing and strengthening these critical international institutions. We tried but did not succeed in doing so in government – for example securing a first Security Council Resolution on Iraq and then working very hard but failing to obtain a second one authorizing force. Much worse, the Conservative–Lib Dem coalition has seemed indifferent. Theirs has been a foreign policy of at very best short-term pragmatism, as well as disastrously sidelining Britain internationally by isolating us within Europe.

Despite recent abject failures of Europe's leadership and the chronic euro crisis, its progress over the past 60 years has been massive: the creation of once unimaginable peace and stability across a continent where more wars were fought in recent centuries than on any other; the promotion of democracy and human rights, especially in the former dictatorships of southern and eastern Europe; and the development of a competitive single market in which social justice and environmental standards have been enhanced not diminished.

The European experience is a remarkable story of how, by sharing sovereignty but still retaining national identity, states can work together to confront common challenges, achieve common interests and thereby become stronger. That is why Labour's willingness to show leadership on Europe will become ever more vital in future. Labour leading at home by unrelentingly making the case that our membership of the European Union makes Britain stronger, safer, wealthier and greener. And Labour leading in Europe, ensuring that together we look outwards to the challenges of this new century: building a world in which social justice, democracy and human rights are spread ever more widely as the key to sustainable development.

But this means Europe must shape, not just react to, international affairs. In recent years, a common approach from the European Union has indeed been playing an increasing role. But the EU has been less influential than it ought to have been as still the world's richest single market. It needs a much stronger EU foreign policy which, however, will not make Britain's weaker. On the contrary, it would help advance British interests in a way that we cannot do alone.

MULTI-POLAR WORLD

With China and India fast becoming economic superpowers – in time diplomatic ones too – and the emergence of the BRICS group (Brazil, Russia, India, China, South Africa), US global dominance is being superseded. Although Britain is too small to exert influence on our own, as part of Europe we can do so. But that means a Europe with a stronger foreign policy mandate and a stronger president representing member governments through the European Council.

The United Nations Security Council also needs reforming so that its membership reflects the world as it is now, not as it was in the colonial age of 1945. It is absurd that Germany, Japan and India are not permanent members. It is ridiculous that neither Africa nor Latin America has a permanent member. Nominally Britain has been committed to such UN reform – except that I recall one of our most senior diplomats telling me in 2000 that it was 'better to travel than to arrive'. It is high time we 'arrived'.

Not that UN reform will of itself be a cure-all for global problems. What it means is that UN leadership will become more representative and that countries now able only to carp from the sidelines will have to take responsibility for solving conflicts and tackling human rights abuses – or face the consequences of failing to do so.

SOCIAL JUSTICE AND GLOBAL STABILITY

Stronger international institutions have to be driven by a progressive purpose. Globalization has brought with it great opportunities for the 'Starbucks generation', but not for the 1.3 billion people who live on less than a dollar a day; for the 30,000 children who die every day due to extreme poverty; or for the 90% of Sub-Saharan Africans outside South Africa who have no access to electricity. To these people, at best, the promise of globalization is totally hollow; at worst, globalization appears to stack already poor odds ever more heavily against them.

The 'globalization of responsibility' must therefore be the cornerstone upon which we work to promote social justice and sustainable development around the world. And our belief in the necessity of this task springs from the same considerations and the same values that drive us to embrace these values at home: our bedrock attachment to the equality of all, regardless of race, gender, religion, nationality, sexuality or disability; and our realization that injustice and inequality breed despair and social ills which affect us all.

It must also mean a renewed effort to tackle climate change. As the 2006 Stern Report made clear, 'business as usual' could see global temperatures rise by five degrees Celsius above pre-industrial levels, leading to massive costs far outweighing those required to place the world on a sustainable agenda and a 5–20% cut in global living standards. And the evidence for Stern is already indisputable: inaction is simply not an option.

But, as Stern also underlined, the costs of climate change are already hitting hardest and earliest on the developing world. And competition for scarce natural resources – which can only worsen with the impact of climate change – threatens future conflict in already unstable regions with further consequences for the rest of us such as mass migration. That's why climate change is both a matter of global social justice and global stability.

Furthermore, we won't be able to achieve global co-operation to tackle climate change against a backdrop of ever-increasing national competition for scarce energy resources. Indeed, the risk that countries attempt to buy their national energy security at the expense of international climate insecurity is high.

But our efforts have been hampered by the failure of Western nations to accept that we are, for a large part, responsible for these problems and we should bear the lion's share of clearing them up. That is why it was never acceptable for the United States, with 5% of the world's population and 25% of the world's emissions, to opt out.

Sustainable development is not about the avoidance of tough choices; it is about making different choices. Sustainable development is not about zero growth; it's about smarter growth and greener growth: about exploiting the massive economic and job opportunities which arise from the need to restore and maintain our environment.

Take for example the need for energy in Africa, where the scale of the challenge is daunting: 17 of the 20 countries with the lowest electricity access on the planet are in Sub-Saharan Africa where 585 million people are without any electricity. (That is fully 100 million more people than live in all the countries of the European Union.) Quite apart from the resulting misery and poverty, a huge number of Africans are therefore without the essential prerequisite for a stable modern society.

The solution lies in harnessing Africa's abundance of renewable energy sources; providing communities not only with light and power, but also with opportunities to generate sustainable and self-sufficient wealth and employment, reducing emissions and thereby reducing serious African food and water shortages.

Without energy, health and social services are non-existent to primitive; educational opportunities are extremely limited; and getting on-line is impossible. Without radical change, the people of Sub-Saharan Africa will be trapped in this vicious cycle, and Western aid will be constantly called upon – like a sticking plaster on a melanoma.

Yet Africa has the potential to go its own way with stand-free renewable energy and to leapfrog the costly grid-based generation, as it has done so effectively in telecommunications through mobile telephony. With the help of EU investment, Africa – instead of being a continent falling behind – could be a world leader in renewable energy, something which foreign private investors have yet to recognize. There is a huge investment opportunity in Africa, for instance in hydroelectricity where only 7% of the potential energy resource is being utilized, and geothermal energy where only 1% is being exploited.

There has already been policy consideration in Brussels to cover the deserts, mainly the Sahara, with solar panels. Remarkably, more energy falls from the sun on the planet's deserts in six hours than the world consumes in a year. As well as serving Africa's needs, the Sahara, being close to Europe, could one day realistically deliver 15% of Europe's electricity.

A significant part of Europe's huge aid and development budget should be allocated to funding a substantial renewable energy investment programme in partnership with private companies. Although the EU–Africa relationship has been one-sided for centuries, global climate change is binding our fates together. We need each other more than ever before in the search for a 'perfect solution' to the gathering 'perfect storm'.

HUMAN RIGHTS, LIBERTY AND DEMOCRACY

But let us also be clear: the values we cherish – liberty, pluralist democracy, the rule of law, justice, freedom and human rights – are not unique to us; they are not solely 'Western' or 'Judaeo-Christian' values. They are universal, enshrined in the UN Charter and the Universal Declaration of Human Rights. We do not seek to impose them on other religions or other regions – for they already share them, as the Arab Spring demonstrated. We simply seek to defend these values from the assault of those who embrace hatred and violence, tyranny and terrorism.

For some on the Left, promoting democracy became indelibly associated with the neoconservative agenda and, by extension, with the war in Iraq. Some deride the notion of extending democracy as the ideology of 'American imperialism', imposing alien ideas on societies with different values and traditions. But just because some neoconservatives have appropriated our language of democracy and liberty that does not mean that we should abandon our values.

'Use your liberty to promote ours', said Aung San Suu Kyi. How can we say to a girl wanting schooling in Kabul, or women wanting to vote in the Gulf, or an Iraqi citizen ignoring the bomb threats and queuing to vote in the early hours, that democracy is for us, not you? I remember such specious arguments being deployed by racists preserving apartheid in South Africa. I don't expect them to be advanced by those on the British Left who joined with me in fighting apartheid.

Nevertheless, democracy, freedom and human rights cannot simply be imposed by military might. Yes – in Sierra Leone and Kosovo, Labour with international support had to resort to force in the face of ethnic cleansing, gross abuses of human rights, mass murder, and aggressive threats to peaceful neighbouring nations. But there must be international support for such action, which tragically there was not over either Iraq or Syria.

Both the values and the mechanisms of progressive internationalism need to be at the heart of Labour's future foreign policy as our answer to 'the perfect storm'.

Chapter 18

A SOCIALIST AND DEMOCRATIC PROGRESSIVE VISION FOR EUROPE

The Economic Challenge

Arlene McCarthy MEP

Between 2007 and 2009 the global financial system experienced its worst crisis in almost 80 years with banks worldwide facing losses of more than $2 trillion. These bad investments by banks forced governments to support the financial system with unprecedented amounts of taxpayer finance, while reduced lending by banks has further exacerbated the recession in the real economy.

In the UK alone the government was forced to take £120 billion in bank shares – the equivalent to £2,000 for every man, woman and child in the country. The financial burden of this recession is still being felt across the UK, Europe and the world.

The global financial crisis in 2008 also triggered recession across eurozone countries. The costs of this recession, with stimulus spending and bank bailouts to head off collapse, have led to rising deficits in many countries. Rising government 'sovereign' debt led to a loss of confidence that these debts would be repaid, causing a eurozone sovereign debt crisis.

In December 2009 Greece admitted it had debts of €300 billion – 113% of GDP, almost twice the agreed eurozone limit of 60%. The picture of Greek debt continued to worsen over the following months and Greek bank and government debt was downgraded by credit-rating agencies.

The debt crisis has continued to unfold in Europe. In Ireland the country's banking system collapsed and its banks were taken under government control, transferring large debts to taxpayers. In Portugal, low growth and a struggling economy have strained the budget. In Spain, the housing boom turned to bust. Banks were left with bad debt and Spain suffered a deep recession and the highest recorded unemployment rate in Europe, at around 20%, with youth unemployment over 50%. Italy is the largest eurozone country to feel the domino effect of falling market confidence, with concern focused on its high level of debt at 120% of GDP.

Of course the long-term reasons for the vulnerability of the euro-zone lie in the design of the euro. While the currencies of the eurozone members were merged, the budgets and budget rules were not. The EU budget is around 1% of GDP, compared to national government spending of around 40% in many countries. The rules that were supposed to bind them, the 'stability and growth pact', proved weak and were not enforced, with even the largest euro members, France and Germany, breaching them.

This structural problem is important, because unlike countries with their own currency, a euro member cannot devalue the currency to help its exports, or print more money to help pay off debt. While in good times that is positive, as it helps control inflation and increases confidence, it reduces the economic levers for a country in a time of crisis.

Financial markets are global, as demonstrated by the spread of a crisis that originated with sub-prime mortgage loans in the USA and then engulfed the world economy. The international nature of markets means one nation cannot respond alone. The G20 helps the major economies co-ordinate reform, but the EU is essential to ensure that European countries can speak with a strong voice in global negotiations and that our open financial markets in Europe are stable and support recovery.

The response to the crisis of the right-wing governments in Europe including the UK Coalition government has been to introduce harsh austerity drives to restore their budgets following the costs of the bailouts, the bill for rising unemployment and the loss of revenue due to business failures.

However, these measures have only been shown to further push costs onto those least able to take it. The poorest people, who rely most on public services, suffer most from the cuts. The average worker is left bearing the brunt for bankers' excesses, while these cuts risk a vicious cycle, as is being seen in Greece, whereby cuts further worsen recession, further lowering growth prospects.

The eurozone crisis is a crisis for the UK economy. Continued uncertainty in the eurozone will mean that UK banks will take a more cautious approach to lending. This means tougher conditions for first-time buyers and mortgage holders and fewer people entering the housing market, combined with rising rental costs.

Savers who have deposits that are regulated in the UK have protection of up to £85,000 for the individual or £170,000 for a couple if their bank, building society or credit union goes bust. The European Parliament is currently working on legislation to increase protection for savers who have deposits in another EU country with a European Deposit Guarantee Scheme.

Pension funds are big investors in UK government bonds. If the cost of buying them rises, and the return on holding them falls, then pension funds won't make the same profits. This could result in a drop in final salary pension schemes and less favourable terms for new pension scheme joiners. Insurance companies also invest this money into government bonds so again any income generated is likely to be lower.

The eurozone crisis matters to the UK because trouble in the eurozone's weaker economies is already destabilizing 'core' eurozone members such as France and Germany and impacting on the UK despite us being outside the eurozone.

The eurozone is the UK's biggest trading partner. Around 50% of our exports go to the 17 countries in the euro and we export more to Ireland alone than to the biggest emerging market countries – Brazil, Russia, India and China – put together.

Recession in the eurozone therefore risks recession in the UK, particularly as the Coalition government is betting on an export led recovery to make up for domestic cuts.

Collapse of the eurozone would mean big losses to the UK. British banks' exposure to lending to the economies of Greece, Ireland, Portugal and Spain together is around £229 billion; 50% losses on that lending would therefore equal UK bank losses of around £115 billion, equivalent to £5,000 per UK household.

Events in the eurozone demonstrate the risks of adopting severe, short-term austerity measures without a plan for growth.

Until business and the markets are given confidence that governments will prioritize jobs and growth in Europe the European economy will not recover, and the eurozone will not be stabilized.

The economic recovery in Europe has ground to a halt. From isolated problems in certain member states, the slide back into recession is now a real issue for all of the EU's economies, not just in the eurozone.

A key reason is the crisis in the eurozone, but the deeper problem is the fear that governments are cutting spending too far and too fast, sapping confidence from the economy. As austerity has been imposed in one country after another, starting with Greece and moving to Ireland, Portugal, Spain and Italy, we have seen recession hit and therefore debt crisis worsen, in a vicious cycle that threatens the whole of Europe.

The EU's economic recovery – whether or not a country is a member of the euro – will rely on the eurozone showing it can solve its structural problems and end the fear of a cycle of sovereign debt defaults and banks failures that could again threaten the financial system. But beyond the need for structural fixes lies the need for economic recovery, as the only way to restore confidence and bring debt down in the long term. Austerity will not solve the EU's challenges. On the contrary it will choke growth.

Structural problems, combined with rising debts since the financial crisis, have been compounded by the failure of Europe's right-wing leaders, including David Cameron and George Osborne, to definitively tackle the crisis. Beginning with Greece in May 2010, followed by Ireland and then Portugal, a series of bailouts have been agreed to provide loans from other member states, the EU and the IMF. Each 'rescue' deal has been combined with tough requirements for austerity programmes, and in each case the initial injection of confidence from this support quickly dwindled.

Despite these attempts to restore confidence, markets continue to lack faith in eurozone countries' abilities to honour their debts in the long term. This is fundamentally because of a lack of growth. EU support has been combined with tough conditions to make deep, short-term spending cuts. Far from making the economy healthier, these cuts are driving the entire eurozone – including its strongest members such as Germany – into recession. Recession increases costs and cuts tax revenues, wiping out any gains from austerity.

At the same time, falling GDP means the relative burden of debt rises. In practice, the focus on austerity without growth has been shown to be counterproductive.

Overall unemployment in the eurozone is up an estimated 11.3% – 18 million – in July 2012, up 2 million on 2011 figures according to Eurostat. Tough austerity measures are taking a toll on economic growth with consumer confidence at an all time low.

The current approach is failing. A collapse of the euro would unleash a crisis far worse than the 2008 financial crash. In recent elections voters in France, Greece and the UK overwhelmingly chose to reject austerity programmes and Europe's youth are taking to the street to demonstrate against a failing economic policy.

The election of François Hollande as president of France has given a new momentum for European social democracy and a rejection of the Merkel–Sarkozy politics which has strangled economics and weakened European societies. In Greece it served to strengthen the right-wing extremist parties and put the country on a dangerous economic course leading to more recession and job losses. Voters are rejecting the ideological approach of austerity only and its high human cost of unemployment, rising poverty and declining public services.

One of the biggest human tragedies and costs of the financial crisis and the austerity approach is the rising level of youth unemployment. Young people across Europe are protesting against the unacceptable consequences for their generation, and the possible scenario depicted by the OECD of a scarred generation facing a dangerous mix of high unemployment, increased inactivity and precarious work.

Youth unemployment has now reached epic figures:

Spain	50.5%
Ireland	31.6%
Portugal	35.4%
Italy	31.9%
Greece	50.4%

As of December 2011, 5.5 million[1] young people in the EU were unemployed, equal to the entire population of Denmark. The International Labour Organization has warned of a 'catastrophic' rise in unemployment among the young if Greece were to leave the eurozone or the eurozone were to split.

The average youth unemployment rate in the EU is more than twice as high as the adult unemployment rate: 22.1% compared with 9.9%.

For the socialists and democrats in Europe tackling youth unemployment is one of the key priorities for the future, we must give our future generations hope for a better future and enable them to play their part in the economy and in society.

The socialist and democratic alternative economic strategy is to relaunch growth, create jobs and promote investment. It is a policy approach that will contribute to ending the crisis and restoring global confidence in Europe's economies with a jobs and growth pact. Labour in the European Parliament is working with our social democratic partners and is committed to fighting for this alternative vision.

It is an alternative strategy based on solidarity, fairness, equality and responsibility. Ordinary people were not responsible for the crisis but greed, irresponsibility and the Conservative government's austerity programmes have exacerbated and deepened the crisis.

The key elements of a social democratic response to the current crisis are as follows.

A FOCUS ON GROWTH NOT JUST AUSTERITY

Budgets must be brought into line but through sensible planning, which maintains vital investment and does not choke growth. The focus needs to be on policies to stimulate innovation, industrial growth and job creation.

Budget cuts should not be made at the cost of killing off investments with growth potential. For countries being asked to make significant cuts, these efforts must not harm investments in education and health care, particularly in countries in severe financial difficulty. The Parliament has also called for the right for social partners and civil society to express their views on European Commission recommendations, be better included in policy formulation and participate in the new economic strategy.

We need to use the revenues from reforms to fund co-ordinated smart investment programmes to foster growth and employment and build a world-class, low emission knowledge economy. Priority investments in human capital, transport systems, energy use, energy security, green technologies and scientific and operational expertise are a key element of this growth programme.

We are committed to a 'European Investment Plan' to create new jobs, the reallocating of EU structural funds to projects to create jobs for young people, and the introduction of a 'European Youth Guarantee' to ensure that young people are not without jobs for more than four months.

A FAIR SHARE TO BE PAID BY THOSE RESPONSIBLE FOR THE CRISIS

The financial sector has continued to pay out bonuses and to make large profits while the taxpayer has picked up the bill.

The socialists and democrats are committed to campaigning for a Global Financial Transaction Tax, so that the financial sector bears its share of the cost of the crisis. This could raise massive public revenues and serve as a powerful weapon against short-termism, speculation and greed in financial markets.

There is a need to target tax increases on the highest incomes, and reverse the dramatic shift in the tax burden from companies to individual wage earners.

Launch a massive crackdown on tax evasion and avoidance, including undeclared work, imaginative accounting and tax havens, based on greater co-ordination and exchange of tax information.

LONG-TERM SOLUTIONS FOR THE EUROZONE

The design flaws in the euro must be corrected; eurobonds would enable eurozone countries to issue common debt, benefiting from cheaper rates due to the low risk this debt would have. Countries could be prevented from running up excessive debts by limiting their access to these bonds to within the agreed debt limits. Eurobonds would protect the eurozone against financial market speculation and cut the costs of financing public debt for every member state.

There is a need for a European Stability Agency to be responsible for management of European debt and to ensure a co-ordinated response to problems of currency stability, including crisis resolution.

SOLIDARITY NOT 'PUNISHMENT' FOR COUNTRIES IN CRISIS

Eurozone leaders have been torn between needing to help struggling countries and wanting to look 'tough' to their voters by setting harsh conditions on Greece and others. They have failed at both. Only by admitting their interests lie together – for example it is German savers who would be at risk if Greece is unable to honour its debts – can we have a constructive debate about the best course of action.

FUNDAMENTAL REFORM OF THE FINANCIAL SECTOR

We must ensure that our economies are not left vulnerable to future financial crashes. We are committed to regulating the financial sector to ensure bankers and traders serve the real economy, rather than serving their narrow self-interest.

We need to complete the reform of financial regulation and supervision to combat speculation, ensure transparency, accountability and systemic stability, abolish perverse incentives and put the financial system at the service of Europe's businesses and citizens.

Finally, Europe must press more forcefully at global level for a reform of global economic governance to put right the global imbalances which contributed to the 2008 financial sector crash.

Labour in Europe believes Britain must engage with our fellow EU governments to jointly build credible solutions to the crisis. We cannot ignore this crisis; the potential negative consequences for British businesses, people and our national economy are too high.

Those on the Right want us to believe that the social ideals we defend, which brought about the most prosperous, peaceful period in the history of Europe, are now the cause of Europe's problems. The truth is that it is the Right's model of financial capitalism, weakening of the state, squeezing of lower and middle income groups, undermining of Europe's industrial base, weakening of social institutions and pandering to the super-rich, which has failed. The Right-dominated European Commission and Council are trying to prop up this failed system, through economic governance measures which make European taxpayers pay the price for years of mismanagement and financial excess.

The social democratic vision for Europe is to create a new era of opportunity. A new era that will relaunch growth, create jobs and promote investment. A new era where Europe's youth will be given the chance to contribute to our society, an era of renewed hope for the future. We have to grasp the opportunity to rebuild a Europe of hope, so that people across the continent can see that Europe does not have to be the cause of their problems, but instead can be part of the solution to them.

NOTES

1. December 2011 Eurostat figures for unemployed people aged between 15 and 24

Part V

WINNING THE ARGUMENT

Chapter 19

WINNING AGAIN

Forging a New Electoral Strategy for Labour

Paul Hunter

INTRODUCTION

No one should be under the illusion that Labour will simply waltz back into power at the next general election. Labour may be ahead in the polls but it will need a historic change in fortunes to win a majority again. The challenge is stark, and immediate.

Labour will need to gain around 40 extra MPs to have a chance of forming a coalition – about the same number as there are marginals. To form a majority, Labour will face the much tougher task of gaining around 70 seats, and to govern alone at least another 10 on top of that (a feat Labour has achieved only twice since the Second World War – 1945 and 1997).[1] A Labour victory requires a uniform swing of around 5% to gain a majority – something which again Labour has only achieved twice since 1945 and the Conservatives once. Not only does Labour need a large swing, it will also be facing a government at the end of its first term. With the exception of the 1970s, parties who win once tend to win again – although there are few precedents with coalitions.

To prepare for 2015, Labour needs to understand how the electoral map is changing and what lessons it can learn from the past. The New Labour strategy was in part based on taking votes straight from the Tories, appealing to middle-class voters, winning in the

South and appealing to aspirational voters at a time of rising prosperity.

For some in the party returning to these themes offers the only way ahead. For others it is the road to ruin. This chapter examines each in turn. Who did Labour lose votes to and which parties does it need to gain votes from? Where are the key seats (after all, it is seats not votes that decide elections)? Is it the middle classes that Labour once more needs to woo? And how can Labour appeal to voters on the economy?

The argument throughout this chapter is that although there was clearly some merit to New Labour's winning formula, the world has fundamentally changed since the mid-1990s. A new electoral strategy will be required for 2015. The reality is that Labour will fight the next election on a very different political and economic landscape from when it was last in opposition. As such, for Labour to win again its electoral strategy will have to be different. Labour therefore needs to learn from 2010, and navigate a different path through the new political environment. There is no room for error. With fewer marginals and a more cynical electorate, getting the electoral strategy right will be critical.

WINNING BACK THE 5 MILLION

Between 1997 and 2010, Labour lost 5 million votes. Historically these votes would have switched to the Tories. However, Labour's lost votes were fragmented, with the Liberal Democrats gaining 1.6 million votes, the Conservatives up 1.1 million votes, and the BNP up 0.5 million. In addition, 'no shows' were up 1.6 million. This fragmentation offers a different challenge to Labour than the one it faced in 1997. Moreover, it is a challenge with significant opportunities if there is a shift back towards two-party voting as a consequence of the Liberal Democrat fall.

Liberal Democrat votes

Poll after poll has seen support for the Liberal Democrats wallow around the 10% mark, their lowest ratings since the early 1990s. This has potentially huge ramifications for the next general election and a future Labour strategy. Looking at Labour's polling today, the vast majority of those who have switched to Labour have been disillusioned Liberal Democrat voters. How much can be put down to mid-term blues is unknown, but many will simply not return following Liberal Democrat U-turns on their most emblematic policies: tuition fees, immigration and constitutional reform.

There are only a few seats Labour can take directly from the Liberal Democrats. However, taking votes from Liberal Democrats in Tory-held seats could play an important part in Labour's success. Gaining from the Liberal Democrat fall alone will simply not be enough, though. A 5% swing from the Liberal Democrats in Conservative–Labour marginals will only reap 33 seats for Labour. This also assumes that Labour will exclusively pick up the ex-Liberal Democrat vote. At present for every three votes Labour is gaining from the Liberal Democrats one is going to the Tories, and this doesn't break down the results by constituencies. Most importantly, all things being equal, there simply aren't enough Liberal Democrat votes in the marginals. Even if Labour was to win all the Liberal Democrat votes it wouldn't be enough to take Labour over the finishing line.

Tory marginals

Labour must therefore also seek to gain votes from the Conservatives. Winning votes from the Tories is particularly important in marginal seats, with each vote denying the Tories one and therefore counting double. While the Conservatives have been losing support in the polls there is little evidence that Labour is taking full advantage. Some hopes have been pinned on UKIP gaining at the Tories' expense. However, it seems unlikely that they will remain on 8/9 points (as some polls have them) at the time of the next election. Futhermore, how they will fare in Labour–Tory marginals is unclear.

Turnout

Another possible area Labour could hope to gain from is those who have turned their back on the political process. For some, this offers a false prospectus for winning in 2015. If they haven't voted in 2005 and 2010 what are the chances that they will vote in 2015? However, voting patterns are at a historic low. Since 1992, the general election turnout has not been above 70%. This should be a matter of both principle and pragmatism for Labour. Lower turnout is much higher amongst blue-collar voters who vote Labour more than Tory. In fact, because of lower turnout, at the last election wealthier voters received around 1.2 votes for the lowest incomes one. The concern is that lower turnout by economic standing could of course become a self-fulfilling prophecy – those from lower socioeconomic groups don't vote, so Labour does not focus attention on them, so they don't turn out as much.

The electoral strategy in 1997 was focused on taking votes mainly from the Tories. In 2015, because of a more fragmented vote, Labour will need to fight on different fronts. This could be resource intensive and difficult to manage. But, it could also offer a way of overcoming what at first seemed like an insurmountable challenge. There are votes to be gained from the Liberal Democrats and increasing turnout, but Labour will still need to pick up votes in the target seats from those who voted Conservative in 2010.

BLUE-COLLAR LABOUR

To win back votes taken by other parties Labour needs to form a coalition of different voters. A central part of New Labour's electoral thinking was that victory lay with attracting middle-class support, and so the party strained every sinew to court their vote. New Labour was right to recognize that the long march of Labour had not just been halted but was in retreat for some time (a trend accentuated by lower turnout). Not only were more people defined sociologically as middle class than working class, but people also self-defined as such.

However, the blue-collar vote still matters. For the first time in its history Labour received more votes from the middle classes than those it was formed to represent. Although Labour saw a decline in support over its 13 years in office from all social grades, the steepest drop was from its 'traditional' base. Support for Labour amongst the social grades DE and C2 fell by an incredible 20 points over the period 1997–2010. By the end of the period the majority of blue-collar voters didn't vote Labour anymore. Meanwhile, Labour's AB vote stayed remarkably loyal, falling from around 31% to 26%.[2]

To focus purely on the blue-collar vote could easily put off many middle-class voters, and would arguably be electoral suicide. However, regaining support of lower- and middle-income voters, whose wages fell at the end of the New Labour period, must be part of the party's rethinking (politically as well as ideologically). A future Labour strategy needs to recalibrate who the party is speaking to, and cannot become preoccupied with the middle-class vote.

KEY SEATS

In elections, votes are important but winning seats is what really counts. All things being equal to 2010, Labour could, in theory, win a majority at the next election by gaining just 87,000 more votes in the right places. This of course is extremely unlikely – elections reflect the national mood. However, the seats that Labour do need to win must be clearly understood for formulating an effective electoral strategy.

New Labour's approach was that the party needs to look south to win a majority. This argument was restated after 2010 by Diamond and Radice[3] who cited the fact that Labour won just eight seats in the two southern regions in 2010. This seems prima facie to be irrefutable evidence for a southern-centric electoral strategy. However, a detailed look at Labour's 2010 performance shows we did no worse in the south than elsewhere. Comparing the percentage of seats won in 1997 to 2010 (or 2005 to 2010) split by region shows that Labour lost proportionally more in the eastern region, East Midlands, West Midlands, London, and Yorkshire and Humber than in the south-east and south-west. A similar picture emerges when comparing votes.

There is also little evidence for a southern-centric approach in 2015. As Table 1 shows, the regions with the most Tory marginals that Labour will be seeking to win are: the East Midlands and then the north-west followed by the West Midlands. Again, the top 100 seats (based purely on votes and which may not be the most winnable places given the different demographic make-up of constituents) for Labour to win are situated in the West Midlands, East Midlands and north-west. There are most certainly seats that Labour need to win in the south but they are not exclusively there.

Suburban discomfort

It is understandable that New Labour focused on winning support in the south after years of being represented as defending only the areas

Table 1

Swing seats by region	Top 100	Marginals
East Midlands	13	8
Eastern	11	4
London	10	5
North-east	1	1
North-west	13	9
Scotland	1	0
South-east	12	3
South-west	10	5
Wales	5	1
West Midlands	15	7
Yorkshire and Humber	9	3
TOTAL	100	46

suffering at the hands of Thatcherite de-industrialization. However, those days have gone. Instead, there is a case for looking afresh at where Labour needs to win. What seems to emerge is that these places tend to be suburban – neither rural nor urban nor exclusively in the north or south. Places such as: Bury, Carlisle, Chester, Dudley, Reading, Stafford and Worcester. Looking at these places at a more local rather than regional level shows that they are neither particularly wealthy nor deprived, nor Labour or Tory. This was something picked up by W.G. Runciman[4] in the 1960s when he showed that working-class identity (and with it voting intentions for Labour) was weaker in suburban areas even for those who would be categorized as working class. This offers a challenge for how Labour engages with voters in suburban towns. Whilst national policy matters, having a vision and policies for suburbia – a suburban renaissance – could make the difference at the next election. A stark picture of how Labour got this wrong was the 2008 mayoral election. A blue ring of suburban boroughs was perfectly formed round the capital and with it victory for Boris Johnson.

Economically, the swing seats tend to be around the middle and at times face different challenges to those current Labour MPs represent. Tory areas have higher rates of employment than marginals, and marginals higher than Labour seats. This is what you would expect given the nature, history and appeal of the two parties. However, it is important to look at their performance over time. Although Labour areas have fared worse, marginal areas have also struggled to increase employment levels. Some 48% of Tory seats have seen a drop in employment rates since 2010; 52% of Labour seats and 53% of the top 100 most marginal Conservative seats Labour will be aiming to win.[5]

Employment is only one aspect of economic performance that individuals feel. The majority of workers have held on to their jobs. However, pay is something which affects all workers. Income levels in the marginal Tory-held seats are above the average Labour seat but many people in these areas are worse off than they were in 2010. Comparing the official incomes data in 2010 with 2011 shows that of the top 100 seats that Labour will be aiming to win, in 41 of them the lower quartile earner is worse off. Median earners, meanwhile, are worse off in 51 of the 100. These figures are not adjusted for inflation, which crudely calculated makes most people (in the bottom half of the income scale) in most of these areas worse off. So while traditionally Labour areas may be suffering, workers in key seats are also feeling the pain of the Conservative's economic strategy. A plan to rectify this must be part of any future Labour strategy.

Beyond the English borders

Labour's challenge is not just to win key seats, but also to hold on to the seats that it has kept since 1997. These seats are not just in England, they are also in the devolved nations. In Scotland and Wales, the nationalists have shown their muscle in the parliamentary and assembly elections, over the period 1997–2010. But, their vote in *general elections* over that period did not increase. However, that could change if voters in Scotland and Wales perceive Labour to be preoccupied with winning seats in England, particularly in the south. The risk is that a backlash beyond the English borders could offset winning some key seats in the south.

WINNING HEARTS AND MINDS – PUBLIC OPINION AND THE ECONOMIC CHALLENGE

New Labour came to power at a time of rising economic prosperity. The electorate were optimistic about the future and the economy.

Real wages were increasing, job security was higher than today and voters were aspirational. New Labour appealed to that aspiration and could make the election about rebuilding public services. In 1997, fewer people ranked the economy[6] (22%) as a top priority, far below the top two issues: the NHS (63%) or education (54%), both of which Labour had strong leads in.[7]

The backdrop to the next election will be very different. Ranked by importance the economy trumps all other issues, consistently seen by around 60% of people as their top priority. It will be *the* issue in 2015, and Labour cannot trail far behind the Tories on it. This will be no easy task. For many, the 'Great Recession' was the fault of Downing Street not Wall Street. Voters still do not place great faith in Labour's ability on the economy. In Lord Ashcroft's focus groups and polls, the main reason why swing voters wouldn't vote Labour was the economy. Labour was blamed for not 'fixing the roof while the sun was shining', and for a legacy of debt.[8] Moreover, the cuts for many voters continue to be the fault of Labour not the Conservatives. For Labour to win over the hearts and minds of voters it needs to turn this around.

Although Labour struggles to prove it can be trusted with the economy, faith in the Conservative's economic competency is on the wane. With the UK economy flatlining, unemployment failing to improve, wages stagnating and the deficit not falling as much as was hoped the electorate are losing faith in the current administration. Polls show that 38% of people thought the Conservatives were best at managing the economy in October 2010; by March 2013 this had dropped to 27%. The problem is that Labour is still behind and to date has made little progress since 2010.[9] As such, Labour cannot rely on Tory unpopularity and incompetence. Governments may lose elections, but oppositions have to win them (see the Tories failure in 2010). The risk is that floating voters may 'cling to nurse for fear of something worse'.

The pound in your pocket

Unlike 1997, Labour's appeal in 2015 will most likely be to the insecure and angry rather than the aspirational. The continuing economic stagnation and rewards for the top earners is impacting the pound in the electorate's pocket. This is arguably having a broader impact than just the 1980s 'one in ten' on the dole who were concentrated in particular areas of the country. Although softened by historically low interest rates, voters up and down the country are feeling the pinch. The question Labour must surely ask the electorate in 2015 is: are you better off than you were five years ago?

This gives Labour the opportunity to lead on an agenda around work and wages. The party needs to rediscover its language on work and pay which is at the heart of its tradition and has popular appeal. Emphasizing this agenda and how it is important to economic growth and reducing the deficit could offer Labour a way of avoiding policy triangulation on such issues as welfare. It won't be all about the world of work, but tapping into the public's sense of unfairness about jobs and pay will be a critical component. What is clear is that returning to a strategy based on rising levels of aspiration and prosperity is not an option in policy terms or politically.

CONCLUSION

Labour faces a huge challenge if it is to win again. It starts from a weak position, needing to win on a scale few parties have achieved. A winning strategy cannot revert back to the New Labour approach of the mid-1990s. Rather, Labour needs to learn the lessons of its failure in 2010 and understand how the world has changed.

It would nevertheless be foolish to abandon all of New Labour's thinking, but the party needs to think differently about the electoral battle ahead. Whilst it needs to win back voters who switched to the Tories, it also needs to ensure disillusioned Liberal Democrat voters turn to Labour. Although keeping hold of middle-class voters is important, Labour must also appeal to blue-collar voters who have turned their back on Labour in their droves. There are key seats that Labour must win in the south, but there are more in other regions. And Labour must win in 2015 at a time when people's main concerns are around the economy and falling standards of living. These challenges not only demand a more sophisticated electoral strategy, but also a more confident social democratic offer that distinguishes Labour from the Conservatives.

NOTES

1. These figures are based on existing boundaries. It appears unlikely that the Conservative's plans to reduce the number of seats to 600 will succeed. If they did succeed the task would be much greater for Labour

2. Ipsos-Mori, How Britain Voted in 2010

3. P. Diamond and G. Radice, *Southern Discomfort Again*, London: Policy Network, 2010

4. W.G. Runciman, *Relative Deprivation and Social Justice: A Study of Social Inequality in Twentieth Century England*, London: Penguin, 1972

5. Annual Survey of Household Earnings, 2010 and 2011, London: Office of National Statistics

6. Even after Black Wednesday and interest rates reaching 15%, the Prawn Cocktail offensive, the abolition of Clause 4 and promises to stick to Tory spending plans for two years, Labour was trailing the Conservatives on the economy in the run-up to the 1997 election. It was only after 1 May 1997 that people had faith in Labour on the economy

7. Ipsos MORI Issues Index

8. Lord Ashcroft, *What future for Labour* (2010) available at http://lordashcroft.com/pdf/25092010_what_future_for_labour.pdf

9. Ipsos MORI Best Party on Key Issues: Managing the Economy

Chapter 20

COMMUNICATING SOCIAL DEMOCRACY

Making it Real[1]

Helen Goodman MP

How can we persuade people that a more equal society would improve their own lives and not that it would mean paying higher taxes for feckless layabouts?

How can we persuade people that government is on their side and not simply an alien 'other' dedicated to bossing them around?

In short, how can we persuade people to vote Labour?

Of course, the first base must be that we present a set of policies which do not have the unintended effect of penalizing hard-working families and facilitating wasteful bureaucracy, but we also need to reconnect with people's actual experience.

We will only persuade people to support us and work with us if we can demonstrate that we have the right approach to tackle the alienation and insecurity in their lives.

Four real-life stories show how equality and active government really can turn things around for ordinary people.

THE FARMERS

It is a snowy day; I am at the annual meeting for tenant farmers on Bowes Moor in a local pub. The hill farmers of Teesdale are a paradigmatic co-operative community living in harmony with each other and with nature.

They do not have a share in the land ownership, but rights of common grazing. These rights and this way of life existed prior to the Northern Rebellion of 1569 and the farmers exemplify what R.H. Tawney called 'the doctrineless communism of the open field system'.

The incomes of hill farmers are low, many earn under £15,000 per year. Those with families claim tax credits. There is a lot of concern that the well-intentioned botanists at Natural England who advise Defra on the levels of stock which are sustainable may take too short-term a perspective. Standards of administration by the Rural Payments Agency on whom the farmers depend for their CAP payments make the Child Support Agency look like a model of streamlined efficiency.

At first glance a conservative approach appears to be wholly empathetic to the hill farmers. Here is a very long-standing community operating on co-operative principles, mutually responsible, and it is this very mode of production which has protected the environment.

The Labour government did not do especially well by these people and we need to think again. The party is too urban and fails to respect rural communities, or understand their skills, and brings its foolish and inappropriate prejudices to debates on rural life. I am ashamed of the way the Rural Payments Agency operated a ludicrously over-complex system. Computer-generated maps bore no relation to actual geography; arrogant officials showed nothing but disdain for their fellow citizens; and I could buy Bowes Moor myself if I had £5 for every time I had been told 'we can't do that because of European Rules'. Finally, we should have stood up to the landlords on behalf of the tenants, because they cream off efficiency improvements in higher rents.

The NFU is currently running a campaign on milk. Their complaint is that from one pint of milk the farmer can get as little as 2p. And they are quite right. This is unjust. It is a prime example of the predator capitalism that Ed Miliband has criticized. We must be prepared to address powerful vested interests and have the intellectual self-confidence to criticize the market ideology under which such practices flourish.

We need to restore a sense of the public interest, which goes beyond market failure.

AGRICULTURAL POLICY AND INTERNATIONAL TRADE POLICY

We cannot *end* government involvement in this community – we need to *transform* it. Without Common Agricultural Policy (CAP) support the farmers would not be able to make a living; farms would be bought up by conglomerates; ranching would take over; the field system would be destroyed and with it the meadows and biodiversity we all want to see flourish. The beautiful landscape is a product of the inter-relation between man and nature. We love it – this is England, we must protect it.

We need to learn how to listen to communities; we need public servants skilled in negotiation, who understand the overall objectives and can act flexibly away from the ludicrous culture of box ticking and targets. In an area without broadband we need to stop the stupid over-reliance on IT and crazy ideas like ID tags for sheep! To win we must show we understand rural communities, which comprise one-fifth of those constituencies we must win – places like Stroud and Sherwood Forest.

At the same time the truth is that food markets are international and we belong to the European Union. Unless we want to go over to an ultra-green self-sufficiency model of production, and no one in the Labour Party is advocating that, we have to have democratically accountable institutions to represent our interests and negotiate solutions. This is called government – or the state, if you like.

And what else do the Teesdale hill farmers need? Well, they benefit from tax credits, village schools, post offices, properly maintained roads, hospitals and all the social infrastructure of the modern world. Only 5% of the population can opt out of the public services and go private. For the rest of us, a major part of the quality of our life depends on well-run, well-resourced public services. Of course, community activity is strong, but it cannot replace high-quality, properly funded public services and government is needed to run these.

THE MINERS

It is a cloudy Saturday afternoon in July; rain is threatening. I am sitting on the platform at Durham racecourse. A huge crowd spreads across the field. There is a fun fair, stragglers of the procession and over 90 brass bands, and banners continue to march down into the field. Ed Miliband is speaking – the first Labour leader to come to the Miner's Gala in 23 years.

The Big Meeting began in 1885 and is rooted in the history and traditions of mining in Durham and across the north of England. The whole day is an affirmation of the human spirit. When a village raises a new banner, it is taken to the cathedral and blessed by the Bishop. Life and leisure are not about shopping – they are about history, music and the values of solidarity and community. It is a family day when money and the media and all the commercial entertainments are totally absent and everyone ends on a real high.

So far manufacturing has not been able to replace mining as an economic driver. It is in the rundown areas of small towns like Spennymoor and Shildon that we have had to struggle against the British National Party. The cause of their rise is easy to understand. In 2005 I opened a new Electrolux plant in Spennymoor– hundreds of jobs, millions of pounds of investment supported by our Regional Development Agency. By 2008 it was closed, moved to the Czech Republic. People don't just feel disorientated; they feel anxious about their ability to pay the mortgage and for their children's future when, as one man told me, he was now the only English speaker on his shift.

And while we have been successful in the political struggle, through sheer slog on the streets and with the support of the churches, the trade unions and the *Daily Mirror*, the truth is we need an effective economic strategy, one that will deliver jobs and a reasonable degree of security.

On the vexed question of immigration from the A2 and A8 since 2001, the first group of people to come from Central Europe were of course refugees from extremely violent situations. It is to our credit as a nation that people were able to make a home here.

With the benefit of hindsight it should have been obvious that giving residence, work permits and access to social security benefits at the same time that Germany and France denied these was a recipe for large-scale immigration, especially given the difference in standards of living, economic opportunities and exchange rates. But the sad truth is that this was unexpected and unplanned. The officials' forecast was for an influx of 30,000, not the 300,000 who came.

And given the very different historic relations, there must be a real question as to whether the same moral and social obligations apply to these groups as to new commonwealth communities.

ECONOMIC DEVELOPMENT

If you were to ask the former miners now in their 60s and 70s what realistic hopes they have for their grandchildren and their futures, they would see three possibilities:

(1) The first is get educated and join the middle class: this is the route bright working-class children have now had for 60 years – grammar school, up and out, the 1944 Education Act, the expansion of further and higher education. For those who had forgotten their history, the Coalition government's policies on tuition fees demonstrate how dependent this is on a benign, socially concerned, active government. We need to have effective policies to ensure that working-class girls in Spennymoor have the same chances as middle-class boys in north London.

(2) But let's be honest – not everybody's child is going to be a university lecturer; the fact is there will also always be jobs like cleaning hospitals or being a bus driver, which need to be done properly and competently but don't 'lead' anywhere. People who do these jobs are perfectly entitled to proper pay, pensions, terms and conditions, decent homes and neighbourhoods. It's difficult to see how this fair distribution of resources can be achieved without free trade unions, a strong legal framework and – yes – active government.

(3) The third option – and one which Labour pursued successfully, though not on a sufficiently large scale, is 'modern manufacturing'; the 'white heat of technology', etc. It requires a strong science base, a high-skilled workforce and partnerships between universities, and public and private sectors. There is a lot more mileage to be had out of this, especially given the need to re-engineer our economy on a low-carbon basis, but anyone who is either unaware of the destruction this present Coalition government is wreaking or fails to understand its significance is living in cloud cuckoo land.

All three options require effective government. Outside London the Regional Development Authorities did a great job in co-ordinating partnerships and planning infrastructure, and effective local authorities can make a difference too.

A recent success demonstrated what is needed. A new light-bulb factory was built by Thorns in Spennymoor. The decision was taken in Austria, but we won because of the incubator set up by the last Labour government to facilitate research and development and technology transfer with Durham University.

Government is needed both to attract foreign investment and also to negotiate a level playing field at multilateral level, so that we have proper environmental and labour standards and a fair trading environment across the world.

THE MOTHER

I am sitting in the front room of a council house with a constituent, a single mum, who wants to talk to me. To keep her three teenage sons, Sharon has three jobs: as a teaching assistant, as a dinner lady and finally as the school cleaner. She wants them to go to a good local school, and came to see me because she couldn't afford the bus fares which are going up by £540 this year. She is not to blame; she is to be applauded. She is not the culprit; she is the victim.

I have lost count of the number of separated mothers who have come into my surgery at the end of their tether because the absent parent is refusing to pay child maintenance, or they are worried that abusive fathers are going to get access to their children (because as far as I can tell the best interests of the child are trumped by the man's right to a family life). The average family break-up causes poorer women and children and richer men. This is a disgrace for which both individual absent parents and state agencies should take responsibility, address it and make changes.

Working-class women have always worked. My great-grandmother was sent to work in a Nottingham lace factory at the age of nine (just as described in Marx's *Das Kapital* Vol. 1). In my constituency there is a light-bulb factory and 90% of the shop-floor workers are women who must fit this around their caring responsibilities. This is why the enhanced maternity rights, equal pay and flexibility won by successive Labour governments are so important.

As the former Archbishop of Canterbury, Rowan Williams, has said: 'the Neanderthal Right regularly blames feminism for the collapse of the family and the menaces to childhood in our culture...There are so often chains of violence and abuse transmitted from the powerless, childish male adult in a situation of deprivation to the still more powerless woman and on to the child; these chains are unlikely to be broken without a clear feminist analysis of cycles of violence and powerlessness – as well as the broader economic transformations needed.'[2]

According to UNICEF, British children are at the bottom of the well-being index, while Scandinavian children are at the top. Yet in Denmark the rate of lone parenthood is the highest. On the conservative analysis this is inexplicable. The reason of course is that in Denmark there is an excellent social support system and much lower levels of child poverty. The welfare state, far from being part of the problem, is part of the solution.

It is simply wrong to deny half the population freedoms and opportunities on the grounds of gender.

The living wage would really benefit Sharon; the cuts to public services, public sector jobs and terms and conditions will affect her badly. She needs to be defended both as a worker by her trade union, but also by us as Labour, since we know that the lion's share of the deficit reduction will be borne by women.

THE WELFARE STATE

For people like Sharon and her children, the welfare state is essential and it has now become quite tedious that rhetoric (on both sides) swamps reality in discussions about benefits in particular.

This family receives child benefit, which is one of the most popular and efficient benefits in the entire system. They receive tax credits and (once the over-complex administration was addressed) these had the excellent result of both lifting 600,000 children out of poverty and incentivizing mothers to work at least 20 hours a week, which had the very positive effect of raising from 40% to 60% the number of lone parents working.

This is not to say that the current system does not need reform. It was obviously wrong – morally and economically – that some householders could receive £1,000 per week in housing benefit, while carers (mainly women in their fifties who save the taxpayer billions) receive an allowance of £55 per week.

There is a consensus that reciprocity and responsibility should play a part in the benefits system, which is why Beveridge's main plank in establishing it was a nationwide mutual system – national insurance contributions.

THE PRIEST'S TALE

I am sitting in the Stranger's Dining Room in the House of Commons – all gloomy, dark-green Victorian gothic, despite the fact that it's lunchtime on a brilliantly sunny day. The young priest who has a poor parish in a multicultural community in central London is telling me about his dilemma. Because of the cuts, the local council is having to close its day centre for old people. This is the place where many old people who live alone can go from 9 till 5. It doesn't just provide lunch and company, it's also a centre for other services the old people need and use. He has been thinking about setting up a lunch club to take its place, which would be staffed by volunteers. He thinks it can run two days a week and his Bishop thinks it is a marvellous idea. But he is furious at being co-opted into Cameron's Big Society. He wants to speak out about the injustice: 'It just won't be the same', he says.

The Tories have made a catastrophic error in their Big Society project in that they have failed to understand that nowadays very many charities work in partnerships with local authority funding and so the local authority cuts damage them too.

One of the rather grating things which politicians of all stripes do is to wheel on churches and mosques when it is convenient as examples of community building – generators of social capital, as economists would say – but then close their ears to the messages the faith groups bring.

Justice is a major claim in many religions. The question 'if I cannot pay my debts why should my bed be taken from under me?' (Proverbs 22:27) is absolutely relevant to thinking about loan sharks today. St Paul's approach involved a radical change; the invitation to redemption was extended from a select few to all – a new principle of equality. 'There is no longer Jew nor Greek, slave nor free, male or female, for all of you are one...'

The churches are at the forefront of campaigns for the aid, fair-trade and debt relief. But Blue Labour's Maurice Glasman in particular has written: 'Labour values are not abstract universal values such as freedom or equality.' If he is making a point about communicating with a large proportion of the voters he's probably right. Examples are better than principles, and even a mental picture is better than a thousand words. But he seems to be saying something more than this: that principles themselves are worthless.

The notion of justice is deeply embedded in our thought. Most people in Britain have a fairly strong sense of justice (certainly of injustice), hence the outrage at bankers rewards, and surely a socialist party would want to work with this intuition, not against it?

Ideas of justice naturally lead to claims for equality and universal rights. Barack Obama has said: 'Through the struggles... we have learned that the longing for freedom and human dignity is not English or American – it is universal and every citizen deserves a basic measure of security, health care, unemployment insurance, a dignified retirement.' He was able to simplify this into the claim 'Yes we can'. And we can too.

NOTES

1. An earlier version of this chapter appeared in *The Political Quarterly*, 82/4, October to December 2011
2. R. Williams, *Lost Icons*, London: Continuum, 2002

Chapter 21

THE PROGRESSIVE NATIONAL STATE

John Denham MP

Ed Miliband's reshaping of Labour as the 'One Nation' party reflects growing support for 'progressive patriotism'. Politicians have always claimed to speak in the national interest of course, but to 'progressive patriots' a strong national story about who we are, and where we are going, is an essential framework for expressing centre left values, ideas and policies.

Thirty years ago, the very idea of a progressive patriotic pride was generally anathema to the Left. To Labour's middle-class supporters, at least, such ideas belonged in the past; politicians who invoked them were toying with dangerous and destructive ideas. Progress, it was assumed, meant a gradual but inevitable weakening of national identities and structures as we moved towards a more global sense of citizenship and the internationalization of state institutions. If we felt uncomfortable as first the National Front and then the BNP appropriated the Union flag, we rarely tried to reclaim the image as our own.

There has been a profound rethink. Many debates, with different starting points, have all reached similar conclusions. It is the similarity of these conclusions that has given progressive patriotism its force. The reassessment of New Labour's economic record has concluded that reliance on opening the British economy to globalization, for example, whilst eschewing any national 'industrial' strategy left the economy dangerously unbalanced, with poor productivity and weak competitiveness. Our productive base was eroded compared with countries with more active states.

Culturally, the reclaiming of national flags – St George in Euro 96 and the Union Flag around the Olympics – has shown the power of patriotic symbols and stories in expressing a modern progressive idea of who we are and want to be. The idea of nation building could provide an inspiration that tortured debates between multicultur-alism and integration have not.

Devolution's success in overcoming initial public apathy to become the framework for broadly social democratic politics has shown the power of progressive national stories. Rather belatedly, the Left has begun to ask what this means for the constitutional politics of England and of Britain.

On many social issues recent governments have wrestled with a range of problems from obesity and binge drinking to poor parent-ing and low educational aspiration which at root reflect how people act. For all the importance of state policies, our stories of 'how people like us behave' are powerful influences on behaviour. Building a nation depends on how its citizens – and the myriad relationships they have at work, in business, community, families and unions – behave, and whether these reflect shared values of the kind of society we want to build.

Finally, fears that patriotism is inherently reactionary have been tempered by a better understanding that national identities are constantly created and re-created. They are not discovered by ever-deeper research into our past. The reactionary and the progressive have always struggled for ascendancy; they always will. We have choices about which parts of our past we celebrate; we can choose to emphasize those things that support a progressive future. We can write the national story we want for the future. And part of that future is the role we want for the state.

When Labour left office in 2010 we no more had a settled view of the state's role than we had had in 1997. New Labour often showed both a crippling lack of confidence in the ability of the state to influ-ence the shape of the economy and an almost oppressive belief in the ability of a centralized, target-driven and top-down state to shape society. Uncertain experiments with consumer choice models of public services (driven by the imposition of 'choice, diversity and contestability') sat uneasily alongside centralized targets. Local gov-ernment in England was largely sidelined. A price was paid for all this. While services improved, they did not always reflect the levels of investment made. At the same time, Labour didn't use its statecraft to reflect and deepen a sense of national purpose. If Labour's state told a national story, it was that Britain was a nation of public service consumers, distrustful of democracy, relaxed about the efficacy of markets, scornful of professionals, unconcerned about unaccountable power and confident in technocratic solutions.

To the progressive patriot this caricature doesn't reflect either the actual values held by British people, or sound values on which a progressive national identity could be built.

So, what sort of state would 'One Nation' voters expects to build?

David Cameron squandered the early potential of the 'Big Society' and 'nudge theory' by linking them inextricably to a shrunken state rather than different type of state. For the centre left, the state is important: to redistribute wealth; to raise resources for collective provision of schools, health, infrastructure and public safety; to provide focus and leadership for the longer term.

And the public have clear expectations of the state. We don't want to do everything ourselves. '*They* should do something', we say. We mostly prefer the certainty of the minimum wage to a life of trade union struggle. We reasonably expect much to be done well.

But we have a strong sense of our rights to be treated with respect, to be able also to get things put right and to have our privacy respected. Above all, we want to be treated fairly in line with a common-sense British view of rights, responsibilities and fairness.

The striking contrast between the resilience of support for the NHS and the dwindling support for the welfare system shows how important it is that state policy reflects shared values. There's some truth in the claim that 'New Labour usually hit its targets but often missed the point'; a sense that 'it wasn't fair', when the way the state worked didn't reflect widely held values of rights, responsibility and contribution.

A PATRIOTIC ECONOMY

The patriotic economy demands an active state that explicitly puts national interest at the heart of economic strategy. Recent take-overs, disinvestments and lost orders have shaken confidence in the assumption that the best response to globalization was to be as open to the movements of capital as possible. Speculative investors delivered Cadbury's into the hands of Nestlé who swiftly set about its dismemberment. Pfizer withdrew much of their research activity after 50 years in the UK. Autonomy, one of the few UK companies to grow from IT start up to £1 billion company was bought by Hewlett Packard who soon disposed of its British leadership. In 2010, the new government decided to award the Thameslink contract to Siemens in Germany rather than Bombardier in Derby. 'They wouldn't let this happen in Germany' said those who felt the British state had abandoned its job.

The banking crisis revealed an economy far too dependent on the financial sector. Investment in research and innovation have been declining, the economy experiences both skill shortages and widespread under-utilization of talent in poorly paid and unproductive jobs. There are few sectors so strong and so well focused on the future that we can be confident about Britain's ability to pay our way in increasingly competitive global markets.

The progressive patriotic state would be actively engaged with private business in shaping Britain's economy. This will require profound change from existing government structures. Perceptive observers are already warning that the Green Investment Bank and any British Investment Bank will simply replicate the failings of the private sector if there is no cultural change in their sponsor.

Understanding that the rules on corporate governance, investment and finance must change is one thing; understanding how to change them, and to make the most effective use of regulation, procurement and long-term public policy to create market opportunities and certainty for Britain's most competitive companies is no easy matter.

This has to be a national mission, not a technocratic policy change. The values of national economic renewal need to be heard in boardrooms as well as on the shop floor, and reflected in the praise given for some behaviours and not others. Individuals will need to develop their skills and grasp opportunities, but we are much more likely to inspire them by appealing to a sense of national effort than with dire warnings that they are on their own in a hostile world.

Ed Miliband has said 'One Nation Labour is a way of taking hard decisions, not of avoiding them'. Certainly only a clear national economic mission will let an incoming Labour government explain why investment in infrastructure, innovation, research and skills must trump the demands from public services and redistribution.

Much of our economy may not be British owned or British head-quartered, but decision makers in global companies nonetheless prefer to invest in countries with a strong sense of national purpose. A progressive patriotic state can help make Britain more competitive in a globalized economic world.

But a strong sense of national purpose can't grow from a wildly unequal economy. If a few take all the gain we won't generate the solidarity needed to succeed. A shared economic mission needs Labour's commitment to economic justice. By emphasizing decent pay and better jobs, 'predistribution' promotes essential fairness and reduces the demands on the state for tax and redistribution. In this way a clear story about the patriotic economy makes the argument for the huge changes – for pay transparency and pay ratios, for the promotion of the living wage and the case for extending trade union representation, for switching the emphasis from tax credits to affordable child care, that Labour should be trying to bring about.

PROGRESSIVE PATRIOTISM AND THE WELFARE STATE

For all the importance of the state, the centre left has often been careless about whether our policies reflect and reinforce popular progressive values or undercut them.

The NHS has a popular resilience which runs deeper than its performance has sometimes merited. (The NHS performance in 1997 was much worse than the health systems of some other European countries but Labour could successfully campaign on '3 days to save the NHS'.) The reason lies in the basic principle of the NHS: 'we all pay in and it's there when we need it'. It speaks to a deep notion of what we want to be like as a nation.

The contrast with welfare could not be more stark. By 2010 patient satisfaction with the NHS was at its highest level ever but consent for the social security system had fallen steadily. Indeed public support collapsed through the economic crisis even faster than the Coalition government has been able to attack it. The needs-based, responsibilities-blind allocation of housing, services and benefits seen as 'fair' by the Left got further and further out of touch with the more rugged British sense of fairness, based on reciprocal notions of responsibility and contribution as well as of rights. The postwar settlement based on a contributory system was, for all its limitations, much more in tune with a popular sense of right and wrong. Notions of 'paying in' and a sense that means-testing punishes those who 'do the right thing' have persisted long after 'the stamp' disappeared.

The progressive patriotic state will have to find ways of rebuilding a sense of contribution and earned entitlement into the delivery of social security and the allocation of social housing and other goods if their values are to bind us together rather than pull us apart.

And the evidence suggests that if we do, people will be more willing to be more generous to those who cannot contribute for themselves.

In other areas, popular sentiment provides a good guide for the progressive patriotic state. People are pretty pragmatic about using private companies to improve public services – using private hospitals to fill gaps in NHS capacity for example. But there is also a deep-seated hostility to the idea that public services in general should be run for profit.

There is a popular notion of a public space, a common good, that lies beyond markets and individuals which is not only deeply held but essential to the notion of a progressive national story and a patriotic state. For a long time, we've been invited to believe that it is only the quantity of the measurable outcomes that really matters, not how they are achieved. That's bred a carelessness about some of the institutions that could defend or manage that public space. Trustee-based pension schemes were undervalued; autonomous universities – legally private but fulfilling a public purpose – are being undermined today.

However, it's very clear that progressive nationalists can't just reflect current popular value. We have to build on the progressive elements of them and introduce new ideas and arguments into the national story. We need to make defending collective provision and the common good part of our national story; a shared aim that helps to bind us together. The progressive patriotic story needs to say that if we all want the common good – a provision we all share and rely on – we all need to take a part in defending the common good.

The same is true in building support for a less centralist state. In the absence of a compelling localist version of our national story, top-down government-designed attempts to create new public institutions have largely left the public cold. Few people wanted elected Police and Crime Commissioners; Foundation Hospital Trusts are hardly seen as popular democratic institutions; experiments with mutuals and co-ops are limited; free schools have come from minority interests of dubious legitimacy; most of England's cities turned their back on the offers of directly elected mayors.

Our opportunity is to write a new story – one which draws on our historic pride in our towns, cities and distinctive regional identities. We need to say, particularly in England, that these values of local pride must be reflected in the leadership of local institutions including those we elect. We should be proud of our community institutions, and voluntary organizations for what they say about the people who created them and about our long tradition of tackling problems for ourselves, not just as subcontracting delivery partners of a centralized state. The voluntary sector needs space to grow and breathe, not just to be a subcontractor of central government.

As with the NHS, the patriotic state needs to create institutions which, by both the values they reflect and the service they deliver, can have an enduring popular character well beyond the existence of a particular government. In a world in which the media is ever more superficial and short term, we need institutions more than ever which 'speak for themselves' and garner and develop their own support.

Rhetoric alone won't do the trick. Revitalizing local government won't work without giving local authorities significantly more power to spare, scrutinize and hold to account all local public spending. Rather than stake everything on a single populist mayoral figure, it might be better to enhance the status and standing of local councillors whose weak and ill-defined roles are reflected in low council turnouts.

And it's not part of our British history to subsume individuals to the collective good. A patriotic state has to be open with its information, its data and its decision making, and the ability of individuals as well as communities to get redress and action taken when things go wrong.

As dissatisfaction grows at the lack of any distinctive English voice within the UK, a radical devolution to English local government looks like the only way to give English people a level of say and control comparable with those in Wales and Scotland. Empowering local institutions can be part of our story of English national renewal within a strengthened union.

MULTICULTURALISM, INTEGRATION AND NATION BUILDING

More widely, progressive patriotism can be the missing element in the debate between multiculturalism and integration. Multiculturalism has fostered respect and mutual coexistence between different ethnic, faith and cultural groups. Britain's experience of handling significant and sometimes unplanned migration compares well with other European countries. But saying 'we are a multicultural society' is an all too vague objective that tells us little about the country we are trying to create. It doesn't provide a sound basis for challenging intolerance, discrimination or separatism. On the other hand, 'integration' – implying that a cohesive society depends merely on the minority becoming like the majority – allows too little space for the fresh, new and different contributions of new communities.

Neither are good ways of telling our national story. Both give far too much emphasis to migration and cultural issues as 'the problem'. In reality our national story has much more often been defined by quite different historical events: from the Norman conquest to the split with Rome; the civil war to the glorious revolution; the Napoleonic wars to the Chartist struggles for trade union rights and universal suffrage; from the twentieth-century wars to the establishment of the NHS and the welfare state. It's an odd distortion of history to suggest that migration is what defines our national identity. What we need is a national story that explains how and why we became a diverse society and, in particular, draws the link between our imperial history and the diverse people we now are.

A progressive patriotism challenges us to tell a new national story that includes the stories of all the peoples who are making their home here, but one which makes our new diversity just part of a much longer story.

In truth, politicians can't dictate this story; it has to be made by people themselves. But the state can be explicit about the need to tell a new national story and can sometimes foster it, as the Olympic opening ceremony showed.

PROGRESSIVE PATRIOTISM AND THE WAY WE BEHAVE

Modern government has become increasingly concerned about problems like obesity, binge drinking, poor parenting and low educational aspirations. Public policy has found it tough to influence the personal behaviours that underlie them. Yet, many teachers in deprived areas welcome those migrant families with high educational aspirations. Our manufacturers look enviously at the respect and status of the German skilled technician or engineer. Atheists may grudgingly acknowledge the greater tendency of faith communities to volunteer and support charities. It seems that stories about 'how people like us behave' are powerful influences on what we do.

If we want to say we are a people whose parents value education above all else then we need both to celebrate those parts of our community for whom this is true and ensure that schools are not slow in challenging those for whom it is not true. If we want to be able to say self-help, good health and sport are important to us – a challenge where the Finns have succeeded impressively – then junk-food manufacturers need to be branded unpatriotic as much as citizens need to be challenged by their own behaviour. This is a shift in language and approach. We are used to persuading people of their self-interest; we are beginning to get used to saying the certain behaviours are selfish and wasteful. We have yet to construct a story around public policy in the national and patriotic interest.

Doing so not only gives us the opportunity to embed technocratic policy within clear values and a national story, it also enables us to draw on the contribution of different communities, making them part of our patriotic narrative.

Some people will respond to this argument by saying that we can talk about our values without talking about a national progressive patriotism; we could put them forward as a universalist social democratic credo. Without doubt, if we believe in our values we wouldn't believe they only apply to us. But we don't live in a universalist world. To most of us, our values really come to life in our everyday lives, and in what they mean to me, my family, my community, and in the country that is my home. That's what progressive patriotism can provide.

Chapter 22

ONE NATION LABOUR AND THE FUTURE OF SOCIAL DEMOCRACY

Andrew Harrop

When Ed Miliband unveiled 'One Nation Labour' it was much more than a daring rhetorical land-grab. For One Nation is an organizing concept that can breathe fresh life into social democracy in an age where class defines and divides us less but inequalities are greater than ever. Today egalitarian politics cannot be sectional, if it ever could. The aim of social democracy is not to advance the interests of 'labour', 'working people', 'the poor' or whatever code-word you wish to use. It must be a politics for the whole nation, for the vast majority, but one which remains true to our enduring values. Social democratic politics should seek to achieve an economy, society and state that works for everyone, building unity in our diverse nation.

A ONE NATION ECONOMY

One Nation is a response from the mainstream Left to the Occupy Movement's call for a politics of 'the 99 per cent'. By defining himself against elites and vested interests, Ed Miliband is seeking to create a broad and inclusive version of Labour's goal of placing economic power into the hands of the many. Creating a political dividing-line between the vast majority and the elite is possible because it is under-pinned by economic reality. One Nation Labour is a reflection of the polarizing structural shifts in the economy which took place over the last 30 years. Even during the New Labour era wages fell and profits increased as a proportion of GDP; median earnings stagnated; pay and wealth differentials accelerated; and households became more indebted as companies piled up huge surpluses. The rewards were amassed disproportionately by a small economic elite, who drew further away from the rest of society.

To Labour's credit the remainder of the economic pie was actually shared by everyone else pretty evenly. Inequality did not widen between the 10th and 98th percentiles of the income distribution, as a result of redistribution plus successful labour market policies.[1] Gordon Brown used buoyant tax revenues to top-up the incomes of people who would otherwise be falling behind, particularly poorer families and older people. The story was similar with education, where the gap between top and bottom closed a little.[2] This was a New Labour version of Croslandism, founded on the presumption of growth and an unchanging economic structure, where equality was to be achieved through the distribution of resources by the state. Yet even in the good times inequality grew worse within the mainstream with respect to health and wealth.

Then there was the financial crisis: past indifference to the super-rich evaporated; the tax revenues to pay for redistribution collapsed; and the Left remembered that the nature of economic growth matters for the wide distribution of prosperity. In response social democratic thinking has shifted from an emphasis on distribution after-the-event to the forging of a new political economy: to reforming both the rules of the game and the spirit in which people play. It is a vindication of the path set out by Will Hutton and others in the early 1990s which new Labour chose to ignore. So far much of the debate has been organized around ugly terms such as 'the squeezed middle', 'pre-distribution' and 'responsible capitalism', which play well in the seminar room but don't cut it with the public. The language of One Nation changes that. It reflects the simplest of propositions; that economic growth must benefit the vast majority not just the elites.

So far the diagnosis has been far better than the prescription, perhaps because the mainstream Left is only slowly coming to terms with the radical implications of moving beyond Croslandite redistribution. Without new public funds Ed Miliband's pledge to stop inequality rising requires a fundamental reordering to turn the UK into a more mainstream Northern European economy. Merely saying 'thus far and no further' on income inequality may sound very timid, when looking across the broad sweep of socialist history;

but the policy solutions imply a radical rupture from the rules and norms of the last three decades, on the scale of 1945.

So building a One Nation economy has implications that stretch far beyond the 'one per cent'. It means tilting the balance in favour of northern Britain; low and middle earners; long-term investment; and manufacturing. But the language of One Nation is an attempt to say you can be 'for' one group without being against another. It is an argument that rebalances matters for the long-term prosperity and welfare of both rich and poor; that after the crisis, the claim of the *Spirit Level* cannot be ignored.[3] Take the example Ed Miliband alighted on when he launched 'One Nation Labour' in 2012, the case of the technical education for 'the forgotten 50 per cent'.[4] He presented this as a prerequisite for long-term economic sustainability, not just a question of social justice. University graduates should care as much as those left behind by education today, because the nation's future will depend on mid-level skills. One Nation is an economic and a moral case for attending to the needs of everyone in society.

A ONE NATION SOCIETY

With the prospects for a rapid reduction in inequality frankly remote, One Nation social democracy has to be about more than economics. Social democrats today must set out to equalize life chances and people's ability to lead valuable lives even in a financially unequal society. This implies that money and personal consumption must become a smaller component in how people in Britain thrive, secure fulfilment and pass on opportunity to future generations. It means focusing on the intangibles – what Miliband terms the 'common life' of culture and social fabric – as well as the value to be gained from public and communal institutions.

So One Nation Labour is more than an argument about rebalancing markets. In my view it is a synthesis of three strands of contemporary social democratic thinking. There is the Left's enduring commitment to egalitarianism, articulated best in the last 60 years by Crosland and Rawls, which informs the One Nation economic agenda. But there is also a strong streak of political and social liberalism; and the communitarianism of the 'Blue Labour' project with its focus on relationships, morality and identity. I've previously argued that Ed Miliband's brand of social democracy is best thought of as an attempt to combine these three intellectual traditions.[5] This is particularly true in the case of society and culture. So when Miliband talks of One Nation he highlights our common life and the impulse to conserve, but stresses liberal values such as openness and tolerance as core to Britain's identity and heritage. This three-way synthesis is exemplified in his attempt to redefine Labour's position on immigration: he argues that the way to reconcile liberalism and social conservatism is for immigration policy to be designed around the economic interests of people towards the bottom of the labour market.

The very word 'conservative' makes many on the Left uncomfortable, though in some respects social democracy is about conservation. If our aim is a united society, then we will wish to preserve values, ways of life and institutions which bring us together as long as they are not based on patriarchy, prejudice or exclusion. But the term 'conservative' is too static and backward looking. It suggests complacency with respect to our inheritance, be that cultural intolerance or the design of our welfare institutions. I propose 'stewardship' as an alternative, since it captures the Enlightenment values of progress and agency, while not dismissing continuity and heritage. For it should always be the Left's aim to build on as well as preserve what we inherit, to pass on something better to future cohorts. Take for example the greening of the economy: we owe it to future generations to conserve our natural endowment, but that means investment and transformation not turning back the clock. It's also an area where allowing a thousand local flowers to bloom is not enough; decarbonizing society can only be achieved with the knowledge, centralized co-ordination and long-term planning of the much-maligned 'expert' who is so associated with the Fabian tradition.

A ONE NATION STATE

So in part the idea of 'stewardship' is a Fabian repost to the recent (mis)characterization of its rich tradition of democratic collectivism as the embodiment of the evils of 'big state'. State collectivism, with its national purview, long-termism and sense of agency, must have an enduring role if we are to create a better society than the one we inherit. Even the Left's communitarians and localists would accept we need political stewardship and the tools of the state to set in train the changes which might promote their objectives of responsibility, shared lives, loyalty, co-operation, autonomy and vocation.

Advancing seemingly 'anti-statist' ends purposefully with the tools of government may seem paradoxical, but the alternative of mere exhortation will always founder, as David Cameron has discovered with his Big Society project. Consider Maurice Glasman's proposal to revive the vocational polytechnic or Jon Wilson's vision of democratic, autonomous public service institutions.[6] How are either to be achieved without 'top-down reorganization' and central agency on a grand scale?

In any case, the communitarian, decentralist version of social democracy only takes us so far. In truth many of the challenges Britain faces require solutions grounded in strong central leadership, not just the flowering of local institutions and solutions. I have already talked about the reordering of the economy and about environmental sustainability, where purposeful, expert, long-termist regulation and intervention is essential. But there are other good examples. New Labour's pension reforms should be held up as a paradigmatic example of One Nation social democracy in the Fabian mould. They embody the spirit of One Nation both in their aims, to simultaneously reduce poverty in old age and to help people in all income brackets save for retirement; and in their means, combining private and public sector responsibility. In setting out to achieve significant planned change over a 50-year timeframe, through small incremental steps, they are quintessentially Fabian. I would argue we now need a similarly grand approach when it comes to house-building and infrastructure investment, two areas where a failure to take a long-term national perspective has led to gridlock.

There is, however, a stronger case for state collectivists to cede ground to the decentralizers with respect to local public services, where values and relationships are all important. For there is a growing recognition on the centre left that there was a hollow core to the new Labour public services agenda. It was based on the twin pillars of central command and marketization, which both forced change from without, based on instrumental sticks and carrots. At the time, this may have been necessary to resuscitate services after decades of decay, but it left little space for autonomy, vocation, relationships and ethos. We now need public institutions where value and innovation comes from within, and from relationships with citizens, in place of machines buffeted by market forces and central dictat. The challenge is how to avoid throwing the baby out with the bathwater. With less of the market will public bodies remain responsive and efficient? Without central control will politicians be able to define national priorities, tackle failure and achieve a degree of uniformity? Somewhere there is a balance to be struck.

These dilemmas about the organization of public services throw up plenty of robust disagreements within the Left. But they are an order of magnitude below the more fundamental question of the scope and scale of the state. Today the Left is being forced to address this issue in a way that was simply unnecessary ten years ago. There is little dissent from the proposition that public expenditure should remain somewhere around the postwar norm of 40 to 45% of GDP. But public spending restraint is unavoidable in the medium term, because the economy is far smaller than anticipated. This is not to endorse the current government's fiscal plans: there is a strong case for slowing the pace of deficit reduction and doing more through tax rises rather than spending cuts. But bringing the public deficit under control is essential, for there is nothing social democratic about passing on rising debt to future generations.

So for the foreseeable future, the prospects for advancing social democratic ends through new spending will be very limited. The Left therefore needs to consider the purpose of spending from first principles and weigh up whether One Nation social democracy implies we should allocate public finance differently. To do this we must assess the various overlapping roles of public spending and consider the extent to which they build a more united society.

For egalitarians, the state is of course a vehicle for redistribution via taxes, social security and services-in-kind. But redistribution as an end in itself is always likely to be a minority taste, with the potential to divide not unite. Moreover, if we aim merely for redistribution, the logic takes us towards safety-net entitlements which will over time degrade public solidarity and support. Indeed, over the last 40 years our gradual shift to ostensibly pro-poor social security has paradoxically resulted in less generous welfare provision for low income groups and a decline in overall redistribution.[7] So the character of spending matters as much as its distributive effects at a given point in time. A One Nation state should aim to minimize the amount of redistribution which is merely a transfer, especially where it is paying for the costs of economic failure, and maximize the share which also plays the role of 'investment' or 'insurance'.

Spending on economic failure includes welfare provision linked to unaffordable housing, preventable worklessness and poverty pay.

When in office Labour did better than is usually recognized to rein in spending of this sort, especially by introducing the minimum wage and successfully helping so many lone parents, disabled people and older workers into jobs. But huge problems still remain. The ultimate prize for the Left would be One Nation economic reforms which could suppress rising demand for public spending. The challenge is to design realistic policies which will achieve this. This might well be possible with the introduction of Living Wages or job creation schemes, but action to reduce rents, for example, could take far longer to feed into public savings.

The next major category of spending is investment in the future. This ranges from capital spending on infrastructure, housing or green technology to expenditure on children, education and science. In principle much of this spending should pay for itself by boosting long-term growth, but the returns usually stretch beyond a spending cycle. This may explain why the UK remains so bad at prioritizing future-facing spending in the face of competing pressures, as exemplified by the halving of public capital investment after the financial crisis. With many other competing priorities, a One Nation state must ensure future-orientated spending is not crowded out.

The final and largest slice of spending constitutes publicly organized insurance. We contribute in the shape of taxes and then receive public provision when our needs are greater or our income reduced. This can either entail the staging of costs over time, as in the case of the state pension and the NHS, or joining a risk-pool against contingencies such as disability. This conception of spending as lifecycle insurance, of horizontal distribution 'from us to us', was a core component of the Beveridge settlement and has remained at the heart of British social democracy ever since. But the Left has lost the habit of talking about the state in this way. It is the most compelling One Nation argument for public spending, in the face of attempts by the small-state Right to push for a narrow safety net.

One Nation social democracy therefore needs to be sceptical about the extension of means-testing. The tussle between targeting and universalism is of course a lively controversy within social democrat debate, with many complexities. People like Polly Toynbee and Peter Kellner want fringe programmes to be means-tested but fight passionately for universalism elsewhere, particularly when it comes to public services rather than cash payments. And often it is not a simple choice between pure universalism and tight means-testing.

There is the 'progressive universalism' of tax credits; the option of tighter or looser 'needs-testing'; and the possibility of 'back-loading' a universal entitlement, as with the coalition's plans for social care. Finally there is the perennial question of whether entitlements should be earned by contribution or at least notionally earmarked to parallel revenue streams, to sustain public solidarity, consent and responsibility.

In tough times, people place understandable priority on protecting the short-term interests of the poor; and perhaps restricting the odd universal entitlement might do little harm at the margin. But any manifesto which makes serious inroads into the principle of universalism risks undermining the One Nation state. In particular, universalism within the 'investment' and 'insurance' functions of the state should lie at the heart of any notion of One Nation Labour.

The debate within the Left on targeting and universalism is really only half a debate, for we obsess about spending but do not focus on tax. A completely flat system of entitlement can be highly redistributive after all, if it is funded by progressive taxation. With very little headroom for achieving egalitarian outcomes through spending, tax reform suddenly takes on great urgency. There are even a range of tax changes which would be both progressive and pro-growth.[8] It sounds like a no-brainer for One Nation politics, especially better wealth taxation and reform of pension tax relief. But the public case needs to be made. With 'no money left' Labour must start to set out One Nation principles for how tax is to be raised as well as spent.

ONE NATION POLITICS

So One Nation means radical politics. It means a political programme that encompasses progressive tax reform, economic iconoclasm, a gradual reordering of spending allocations, public service reforms that are rooted in values not just results, and identity politics based on liberalism as well as community.

None of this is compatible with mushy trimming towards the cautious views of an imagined swing voter. Rather One Nation Labour needs to be a politics of conviction. The Labour Party has to set out why a radical but uniting version of social democracy is the only way to bring together the vast majority and reflect the perspective of every corner of Britain. With such conviction, leadership and purpose the party will win round many who are ambivalent about Labour today.

The point of One Nation Labour is not to dilute social democracy by stretching to the Right. For in our low-turnout, first-past-the-post democracy, it is possible to govern with the support of less than 30% of adults. The votes Labour needs come from people on the Left of the political spectrum.

But a sectional victory will not buy the legitimacy and permission needed to implement radical change. People who will never vote Labour must still give their tacit consent so Labour can become a party of national leadership in the fashion of 1945 and 1997. Social democrats will only prevail over the status quo and the vested interests if the vast majority believe we reflect their interests too. One Nation is the route to a majoritarian politics of the Left.

NOTES

1. J. Cribb, R. Joyce and D. Phillips, *Living Standards, Poverty and Inequality in the UK: 2012*, London: Institute of Fiscal Studies, 2012
2. C. Cook, 'Poorer children close education gap', *Financial Times*, 1 October 2011
3. R. Wilkinson and K. Pickett, *The Spirit Level*, London: Penguin, 2010
4. Speech to Labour Party Conference, 2 October 2012
5. J. Denham (ed.) *The Shape of Things to Come*, London: Fabian Society, 2012
6. J. Wilson, *Letting Go: How Labour Can Learn to Stop Worrying and Trust the People*, London: Fabian Society, 2012
7. *Divided We Stand: Why Inequality Keeps Rising*, OECD, 2011
8. J. Mirrlees et al., *Tax by Design: the Mirrlees Review*, Oxford: Oxford University Press, 2011

Index